THE
SHARKBITE
METHOD

Nick Kraus with Kelsea Cap

THE
SHARKBITE
METHOD

A *Killer* Digital Marketing Strategy

Discover the digital tactics
every brand should be following

Contents

A shark's bite has several layers of teeth that are always regrowing, making it an apex predator that has evolved to effectively catch its prey. Similarly, *The Sharkbite Method*™ has several layers of dynamic tactics that have evolved over time. The goal remains the same—to catch your target audience's attention and never let it go.

Introduction
Proving the Naysayers Wrong

I had no money left to my name. I had a mortgage to pay, a baby to feed, and $55,000 in debt from the business. Maybe the naysayers were right...I could never start a successful business, especially in such a difficult economic climate.

I was young and could have easily gone back to the corporate world. But I decided to double down on the debt by taking out an additional $55K loan. One thing was different: I was committed to partnering with my clients by providing regular marketing support that would deliver undeniable value. I also knew the best way to prove our services worked was by having an amazing case study. And who better to prove it than with my own company?

Fast forward a decade, and the risk was worth it. We now have offices in multiple cities and have been included in the Inc. 5000 fastest-growing companies list several times. The road to get here has been long and full of learning curves that helped us develop one of the most impactful marketing strategies available: *The Sharkbite Method*™.

I started my career right after college as a packaging designer for Philips, a consumer electronics product company. Because I liked marketing strategy just as much as the visually creative part of the work, I eventually moved into marketing management and product development.

This was a big promotion for a graphic designer with a bachelor of fine arts, but my hiring manager, John, had full confidence in me. Of course, there were also plenty of naysayers who claimed I wouldn't be able to make the transition from designing boxes to managing multi-million-dollar business lines.

I admit, I thought they might be right; I could barely manage my personal cash flow that included a car lease and a one-bedroom apartment. How would I manage a product line with hundreds of SKUs and an eight-digit P&L?

The position was high pressure. Soon after I started, we had a strategic planning meeting with every marketing manager in attendance. We were to discuss the sales forecast for the year, our projected revenue for our respective product categories, and how we would distribute those revenues across the different channels: wholesale, retail, and online. We were also to talk about any new products we wanted to develop.

I had been given the landline telephone and accessory product line and was supposed to tell everyone how the line would decline in sales because, let's face it, landline phones were a dinosaur of a product. Instead, I said, "I think we're going to grow." I presented a plan that John and I had created. It showed how we could reposition the product line and our company into providing the most efficient number of SKUs to maximize the retailer's space and revenue.

Traditionally, companies positioned their product line as "We can provide you with 150 SKUs—everything from wall plates to landlines to cordless phones in white, yellow, and black, along with every replacement battery you could use. We can fill out this category for you in a very detailed way, and that's why you want us."

I said that version of positioning should go away because we know that landlines are being phased out and cell phones are being phased in. It was 2005, so it was not a surprise that few people would be using a landline in the future. I recommended that we reposition Philips as a company with the most efficient planogram for your store that would maximize revenue and profits and give you back valuable shelf space.

I then developed detailed strategies by looking back several years at how many products were sold, the profit margins, and forecasted sales per product item. Analyzing data has always come naturally to me. That data allowed me to devise a smaller planogram that took up less wall space. In addition, we were able to pick the most popular

SKUs that generated a similar top-line revenue and a larger profit margin than before.

So, we gave back wall space, allowing for other product categories that would generate more revenue. I forecasted that my product category would increase sales because we would get new clients—and that's precisely what happened. Walmart was one of the biggest. (We got them in year one. That was a huge win for me.)

They next entrusted me with building out a cell phone accessory product category. We discussed positioning and strategy again, and the naysayers said, "Nick, we will never compete with cell phone accessories because the only place they sell them is Best Buy and we cannot beat incumbent vendors." I said, "Yeah, but when you have time to go to Best Buy is not when you need cell phone accessories. You need headphones and chargers when you're on the move, so we should put them in every drugstore, every gas station, and every airport." We did and created a $10 million category in year one with just ten SKUs made up of cases, chargers, and headsets. It was a multiple SKU, multiple product approach with a small landscape sold everywhere.

That was a brand positioning play, but I realized there was simplicity in supplying a service or product for an unaddressed need, a topic we will discuss later in the book. For the landline product category, the need was a smaller planogram. With this one, the demand was for cell phone accessories on the move, as lots of consumers didn't have time to find a Best Buy.

From Philips to Full-Time Freelancing to Kraus Marketing

Times got tough with Philips in 2008, and I decided to leave the company. Even though they wanted to keep me on, it would require moving to another state, which wasn't in the cards.

I had been doing freelance graphic design since I graduated college—that's how I started with Philips. I would work all day and then come home and do my freelance work from 6:00 p.m. to midnight. When I left the company, I made $50,000 in sales annually from my freelance work, mainly creating logos and websites for smaller businesses.

I soon realized that many small to midsize companies had no reasonable access to a reliable graphic and website design agency. Because several clients needed weekly or monthly work, I started freelancing full-time. I had always wanted to be my own boss, and this allowed me to fulfill that dream. It was not a perfect time, mind you—there never is—but this was the Great Recession, one of the hardest economic times our country had faced in a century. This move led to the naysayers giving me unsolicited advice over and over about how it was ignorant, unintelligent, irresponsible, and impossible to start a company in such a terrible business climate—but I figured it was as good a time as any.

My priority was to start selling as much as I could. I quickly realized that I couldn't sell and do all the work to grow the business myself, so I hired my first employee, Nick Westcott, who is still with the company today. Westcott did our graphic and web design. I also outsourced some of our website development because it was so time consuming.

The team continued to grow. I hired a few more employees and named the company "The Kraus Group," later changing it to "Kraus Marketing." (More on the reason for the change in chapter 3.) Now I've created an engine that has to sustain itself. I have salaries to pay, so I need a steady sales flow.

Admittedly, the first five years were traumatic—an emotional rollercoaster—but that's true of anyone who starts a business. Although many people see it as "You're starting a business. That's awesome. You must be having so much fun," it's quite the opposite; at least it was for me.

I needed to focus on marketing Kraus to get enough sales to sustain the salaries I had committed to paying, and I'm proud to say that I never missed a payroll. I realized that marketing and a steady flow of leads and sales were essential to ensure I could do that for my team.

We continued creating logos and building websites. At the time, convincing people that websites were critical to the sustained growth of their marketing was challenging. The typical comment from the naysayers was, "I understand that some companies need a website, but having a website doesn't make sense for my company." Remember that this was 2008, and many generations were still not using the internet regularly. To prove the value of a website, we started measuring visitors, time on site, and creating case studies to show our clients.

We became experts in Google Analytics, the gold standard in website analytics, and connected all our sites to it. We started helping clients understand that hundreds and thousands of people visited their website every month. Just because they didn't hear about it did not mean it wasn't happening. We had the analytics and reporting to prove it. Tracking these metrics helped our clients understand their website's importance and why they should keep it updated.

I recall showing the owner of one of our clients, a commercial developer who built dozens of apartment and condo buildings in northern New Jersey, their site's analytics. The owner was a successful businessman in his early sixties who thought he should give up on the website because, in his mind, it wasn't delivering any value.

However, once I showed him the number of visits he received, he quickly understood the need to continually drive traffic to the site and keep it updated to reflect the new buildings the company was constructing and the newly available units. This was an early win for our company: we had proven value, and for that reason, our client would continue to invest. That investment would provide an ROI for the client and sustained business growth for Kraus.

Our next step to provide value was improving visitor traffic to our clients' sites, so we focused on search engine optimization, or SEO. Showing up on search engines like Google was easier at the time, but many clients did not understand the importance of doing so and again said, "I understand why some companies need to show up on Google, but no one is searching for our products or services online." I still hear naysayers say that to this day.

Our first SEO success was for the keyword "kitchen contractor near me." It was for a local kitchen contractor who needed our help. We got the site to rank number one throughout northern New Jersey. They received enough inbound leads that the company had to create a whole new sales system to keep up.

I also did this for Kraus Marketing. We used the keyword "website design company." I decided not to use "agency" because I thought people would type "company" into search engines more than "agency." We were right and reached number one for that keyword. It quickly delivered a dozen leads per month.

I admit that it was relatively easy to rank highly back then—we're talking 2009, and times have changed drastically since—but mastering SEO was another huge win, another notch in the belt. I have always been intent on doing the right thing for our clients, and SEO (although hard to sell) had proven its worthiness in our company's tool kit. We started doing SEO for all our clients as an integral part of our service offering.

We built the websites. The analytics helped our clients realize how important it was to optimize their sites. Then we used those analytics to show them the value our SEO services were providing to their website.

Next, we began looking into adding social media marketing as a service line. I still remember hearing on the national news about a pizza restaurant in Florida that used social media for marketing. They posted on Twitter that if you mentioned the tweet when you ordered, you could get 50 percent off the cost of your pizza. It created a line down the street. That led to a nationwide news story about how business owners now use social media to advertise their companies. A light went off in my head: How have we not utilized this yet, and who can we use it for?

I called a meeting with the owner of the commercial development company mentioned earlier and talked to him about how I thought Facebook could help him sell more condos. The thought of using Facebook made him chuckle. I still smile endearingly when I think of how he laughed; it was raspy from years of smoking. After he was done laughing, he said, "You want me to put my condos on Facebook!?"

Despite his skepticism, he trusted me, and we started using Facebook to help showcase his buildings. We created Facebook pages for each development and posted about the building amenities, low mortgage rates, and wonderful opportunities to live downtown. Those posts helped drive enough awareness and traffic that the company lowered its spend on traditional marketing like newspapers and billboards. Instead, they moved that budget into social media marketing.

With these continued wins, I started teaching clients and doing speaking events to prove the naysayers wrong—digital marketing works. In the years since, I've been lucky enough to travel around the country and talk to many different industries, telling them in sixty- and ninety-minute sessions how to create a sustainable, manageable program that can change their business. I felt it was a way to educate my target audience and give them the marketing tools needed to gain more clients.

Those stories are just the iceberg tip of the many things we've done throughout the years that enabled us to grow our company by double digits year over year and continue to help clients do the same for their companies.

In 2016, a multi-location regional retail brand approached us with the need to revive their company using the same holistic digital marketing approach we discuss in this book. They found us while searching for marketing agencies on Google and told us they read the blog posts we wrote weekly.

The retailer was advertising with Valpak and through other traditional marketing methods firms, and competing online stores were taking their sales. The company's revenue had decreased steadily, from $20 million in annual sales to $9 million when they came to us. We helped them go fully digital with their e-commerce; got them started with social media, email marketing, and SEO; and created a solid digital presence across multiple channels.

That was our first understanding of how important it was to use these tactics together, proving the whole is greater than the sum of the parts. Using each tactic separately resulted in incremental improvements; by using them together, growth was exponential. The company went from declining revenue to a sales increase of greater than 30 percent that same year: $12 million.

From there, we started getting referrals from larger and larger brands. We're lucky to work with some of the country's biggest companies, curating a Fortune 500 and Fortune 100 client portfolio.

Out of those learning experiences and growth opportunities, we developed a multipronged approach to digital marketing that we call *The Sharkbite Method*™.

What You Can Expect from Reading *The Sharkbite Method*™

Why I Call This Book *The Sharkbite Method*™

For more than a decade we have been developing this killer digital marketing strategy. *The Sharkbite Method*™ builds brand value, shortens sales cycles, drives leads, and creates revenue.

A shark's bite has several layers of teeth that are always regrowing, making it an apex predator that has evolved to effectively catch its prey. Similarly, *The Sharkbite Method*™ has several layers of dynamic tactics that have evolved over time. The goal remains the same—to catch your target audience's attention and never let it go.

The Purpose of *The Sharkbite Method*™

This book aims to teach emerging midmarket and large enterprise companies how to use digital marketing successfully, including how to staff a marketing department, build brand awareness and value, shorten sales cycles, and generate leads. If you're a small business, the strategy will still apply; however, bandwidth may become a challenge.

The goal is to empower readers to learn what a successful marketing campaign can do for their business and teach readers how to apply a proprietary multipronged marketing approach that my team and I developed over the years. Ultimately, it is to give each person a marketing strategy to help them grow their business.

Who *The Sharkbite Method*™ Was Written For

The primary audience for *The Sharkbite Method*™ is chief marketing officers (CMOs) and marketing directors. They know brand strategy and its purpose but not the exact tactics of marketing digitally.

It's also intended for CEOs and business owners who are embarrassed about their digital presence and need to get inbound leads but lack "how-to" knowledge.

Lastly, it's for second-generation owners—those next in line to take over the family business. They are open to marketing and know its value but don't necessarily know a lot about it and the strategy involved in its execution.

What You Will Learn by Reading
The Sharkbite Method™

The Sharkbite Method™ can be easily broken down into three segments: the foundation, the execution, and next steps for maintaining your success.

Part I (Chapters 1–4)—*The Sharkbite Method*™: Strategy Development

What a business needs to build a solid digital marketing strategy.

Chapter 1: Evaluate Your Marketing Needs

Gain insight into how businesses can identify their marketing challenges and opportunities. Companies can achieve better marketing efficiency and effectiveness by addressing internal and external marketing support and by defining roles and responsibilities.

Chapter 2: Goal Setting to Brand Positioning

To make the most out of the tactics and strategies discussed in this book, this chapter helps businesses determine their most important growth goals and desired brand positioning.

Chapter 3: Develop the Creative Brief

A creative brief is central to any marketing campaign. This chapter helps marketers understand what a creative brief is, its importance, and how to develop one for use in a marketing campaign.

Chapter 4: The Importance of a Content Calendar

Here we focus on the importance of creative and campaign messaging, how to develop a successful campaign, and strategies for determining the right audience fit. This will act as your guide throughout your marketing campaign.

Part II (Chapters 5–9)—*The Sharkbite Method*™: Strategy Execution

The book's main body outlines *The Sharkbite Method*™ strategy and tactics we use at Kraus Marketing and that we recommend to others.

Chapter 5: Optimize Your Website to Increase Conversions

We point out that a brand's website is the epicenter of all digital marketing activities and should be optimized to achieve the best results.

Chapter 6: Drive Visibility and Growth through Search Engine Marketing

Search engine marketing (SEM) is crucial in building effective digital marketing campaigns and strategies. We examine organic and paid SEM and discuss how it impacts businesses in terms of visibility and customer acquisition.

Chapter 7: Leverage Social Media for Effective Digital Marketing

Emphasizing the vital role of social media in marketing, we guide toward selecting suitable platforms, differentiating between paid and organic content, understanding the features of the most popular platforms, and the principles to follow for optimum use.

Chapter 8: Harness the Marketing Power of Email

We highlight the significance of a reliable digital marketing tool—email marketing—explaining how it fits into a holistic campaign development plan.

Chapter 9: Amplify Your Strategy with CTV and OTT Media Buying

Learn about CTV and OTT media buying, understanding key terminologies, pros and cons, and best practices to leverage these emerging marketing platforms.

Part III (Chapters 10–13)—*The Sharkbite Method*™: Monitoring and Enhancing Your Efforts

The final phase of *The Sharkbite Method*™ discusses how you can maintain the success of your marketing efforts through key performance indicator (KPI) measurement, data insights, proper team assembly, and the power of AI.

Chapter 10: Digital Marketing Measurement and Campaign Optimization

This chapter stresses the importance of measuring KPIs and the return on investment to evaluate campaign success. Discover which KPIs are essential to track and the best methods to do so.

Chapter 11: Understand Your Internal Data and Customer Insights

Evaluating internal data and customer insights is crucial to a successful digital marketing campaign. By understanding the significance of this process, marketers can make informed decisions and create targeted strategies based on objective data and customer preferences.

Chapter 12: Assemble the Right Team

Learn the steps that chief marketing officers and directors can take to build the right team for successful digital marketing campaigns.

Chapter 13: Utilize the Power of AI

Better understand how the integration of AI in today's digital marketing landscape impacts the many processes needed to run a successful campaign.

Are you ready to apply a practical digital marketing strategy to grow your business? Read on!

Part I
The Sharkbite Method™: Strategy Development

What a business needs to build a solid digital marketing strategy.

Chapter 1
Evaluate Your Marketing Needs

The reason your company struggles with its marketing efforts likely has to do with several factors. This chapter aims to equip companies with the knowledge and tools to understand the challenges and opportunities in their marketing landscape. Companies can achieve better marketing efficiency and effectiveness by addressing internal and external marketing support and by defining roles and responsibilities.

Many companies have challenges keeping up with their marketing needs. Challenges relate to what the company is currently doing that demands marketing support. Typically, those challenges center around staffing bandwidth and capabilities.

By bandwidth, we refer to someone on staff who can do a specific job, like copywriting. However, the company's marketing may require more copywriting than that employee can handle. So that's a bandwidth challenge.

Regarding capabilities, this is when the marketing team needs work completed that requires particular expertise but doesn't have anyone in-house. Finding someone with a specific set of capabilities can be difficult, and that's a capabilities challenge.

There are also opportunities. You might identify an opportunity for your company to boost awareness, build value, or create leads. But, again, you don't have the team members available to champion this opportunity.

Think of challenges when evaluating your current needs and opportunities for the future. That's the first step—taking a thirty-thousand-foot view of where you stand.

Internal vs. External Marketing Support

Companies' biggest challenges are the bandwidth and capabilities to support internal and external marketing efforts. By internal we mean support for the sales team, human resources, or other departments. Typically, internal marketing requires shorter turnaround times and is less strategic, more reactive, and company culture focused.

Examples of internal marketing support could include internal emails, sales sheets, presentations, events, and event invites, to name just a few. It could also be as simple as updating the website's "team page" with new employees or posting company outings on social media.

Conversely, external marketing is more strategic and intended to boost brand value, build awareness, and meet demand generation goals.

Here, your marketing efforts are strategic and focus on a targeted audience. It's typically more efficient and planned months in advance, as opposed to the reactive nature of internal support. When looking at your current needs, internally and externally, understand that both are important. It's just a matter of determining the challenges and opportunities for both parties.

However, the inconvenient truth is that, often, internal marketing requires so much support that it leaves little time for strategic marketing, a factor that applies to larger organizations especially.

The marketing team is typically overwhelmed with internal marketing support requests in larger organizations. For example, large companies have bigger sales teams, sometimes running into tens or hundreds of salespeople. There are also huge human resources teams that have many needs.

The sales team wants support for the webinars they just came up with this week. Or they have a new presentation and pitch meeting that must go to a client that could be paramount to the growth of the business, so you can't ignore it. Or they have a social media post that has to happen today, but they don't have the artwork or the approval to make the post, so marketing has to do it for them. Then they request you write an email to follow up on an unplanned event that, again, you're reacting to.

You can't ignore the sales team's marketing needs because many of these salespeople are the largest revenue generators for the company. The same goes for the head of HR.

When the head of HR says the website needs a new culture page or requests to update the team page, the marketing team reacts and gets it done. A friend of mine works in-house at a large corporation as a graphic designer. He once had the head of HR come to him with a last-minute request for an upcoming event she needed help with. Of course, the event date had been planned for six months, but the request came in forty-eight hours before the dictated deadline.

She said, "I need this event on our website, and I think we should make a special logo for it. Oh, and we have a fifty-thousand-square-foot building, and since our signage isn't good enough, I want eight signs throughout the building, but I need them custom designed because the event is luau-based." The lack of planning caused chaos for his next two workdays. He also had to put off other work because he simply couldn't get everything done. The HR director was abusing her power because the company was set up in a way for her to do so.

Pro tip: Creating roles and rules is the best way to have a proactive, efficient, cost-effective marketing team that produces an ROI.

Roles and Rules for Internal and External Support

One of the ways to shift the marketing balance from internal to external is to set up roles and responsibilities. Some employees handle internal requests, while others support more strategic work.

For example, you can have a graphic designer assigned to handle all the LinkedIn posts, landing pages, and sell sheets for the sales team. Typically, that's a junior role because throwing these together is easier and turnaround times have to be quicker. They are less important to the company's branding and they get a lot fewer views.

On the other hand, strategic creative with large media buys behind it should be done by a senior designer with a wealth of experience that will offer the best likelihood of an ROI. Simply defining your employees' roles can ensure you don't have a senior employee pushing off a strategic deliverable to comply with a leader from a different department.

Then there are rules designed to get everyone on the same page. Rules provide the guidance and leadership a team needs to function well. It's basic groundwork stuff, but many companies don't do it.

We once had a very large client stop our retainer agreement because they could not get their act together. Why? They had undefined roles and no rules in place.

The company—a professional service firm—suffered from extreme workloads. Despite having thirty in-house marketing professionals, they were unable to keep up. That's common in a company with thousands of employees and hundreds of salespeople.

In addition to the work (or perhaps because of it), the marketing department experienced high employee turnover. In eight weeks, they lost four team members—two graphic designers, a copywriter, and an SEO specialist—from a thirty-person team that was already shorthanded. When we spoke with them, we discussed that we could fulfill their bandwidth and capability challenges. They thought we were a perfect fit. We thought we were too. However, we found a highly disorganized department once we got started.

Typically, the first step when we begin a client engagement is to have a kickoff meeting. For large organizations, it's a best practice to come in with a fifty-to-seventy-slide PowerPoint presentation that presents everything from their brand history and current brand guidelines to their unique selling points and value props. Other topics include branded messaging, digital advertising, current and past creative, and upcoming projects and initiatives.

In this case, the client had six people present in the meeting: the CMO, the marketing director, the creative director, and three support staff. We had a team of eight dedicated to their account who were ready to immerse themselves in the brand. However, there was a problem. Despite us outlining what we were looking for to successfully run with their requests, they showed up with nothing to give us. Not only that, but they had failed to fill out the prework questionnaires we sent to start the conversation.

So, even with two large teams with very high hourly wages in the room, we had nothing to discuss. They had no key initiatives, upcoming projects, centralized departmental goals, priorities, creative calendar, or future planning—nothing!

We spent three hours trying to pull what they were working on from them. We knew the tactics most companies their size worked on, so we ran through those, asking them what they were doing in each area. Their answers were general in nature and lacked insight. Other warning signs also came up in this meeting.

We learned they had brand guidelines they didn't like and wanted to break. That was a red flag for us because our job was a bandwidth one. Brand guidelines (like font sizes, imagery, messaging, colors, and other brand-related elements) create efficiency because you can do a lot of production quickly when there are rules preidentified for you. But when you want to break the guidelines all the time, production becomes a creative exercise, which takes much longer.

Once we started with their account, we realized they were just sending tasks—create a LinkedIn ad, edit this video, design a one-off brochure—which did not allow us to manage any projects. We thought, okay, once things get going, we'll have more ability to offer our expertise and manage the workload on their behalf. (That's why companies hire agencies like ours.) That did not happen, so we suggested holding regular meetings to discuss what's going on week in and week out to take on larger projects and manage reoccurring tasks on their behalf.

Despite our insistence, they thought meetings were wasteful and preferred emailing daily requests with same-day deadlines. While last-minute work is necessary at times, having this as a regular occurrence is highly inefficient for a team like ours. Our production schedules are typically planned seven to ten days in advance.

To make matters worse, there was a litany of other issues. There were no roles; no one on their side owned any one task or tactic. The art director and creative director couldn't agree on brand guidelines and design. There was no shared vision, and neither had final say, despite the hierarchy of typical titles.

We realized they did not have a turnover and capabilities challenge; they had an organizational problem, so it was no surprise that employees quit left and right. After twelve months of working together, we agreed it wasn't a good fit. (To our detriment, we also realized that if you allow a client to walk all over you, their culture can become yours—and it quickly did, at least for the team assigned to that account.)

Three Marketing Department Best Practices

One: Create Roles and Responsibilities for Each Marketing Employee

This is a best practice for management in general and definitely applies to your marketing department (large or small). If your employees have a clearly defined set of roles and responsibilities, then they can be held accountable. That is why during our employee onboarding and biannual employee reviews we go over their roles and responsibilities. The roles and responsibilities are in writing. It is a bulleted list, detailed and specific. This also applies to your freelancers and outside agencies. With regular communication and conversation, it is unlikely your employees or vendors will swim outside their lane.

Two: Establish Rules to Set Expectations across the Organization

Many marketers allow sales and human resources staff to make last-minute requests. That's particularly true of the head salesperson who, if not given what he wants when he wants it, could get upset and jump ship. So, if Joe needs this or Linda needs that, just get it done.

When assigned a last-minute task you might ask, "Did Joe not know this was coming?" Yes, they knew, but their implied reason for fulfilling their demands is "they just made $10 million in revenue for the company." While internal marketing support is essential, if the stakeholders do not implement rules that require proper planning, then work can become chaotic. To fix this, having a set of rules written and supported by leadership is paramount.

Some of the most typical rules are around timelines, for example:

- Three-business-day turnaround for a social media post
- Ten-business-day turnaround for a website landing page
- Next-business-day turnaround for anything deemed mission-critical
- I've also seen rules that include items like the following:
  - Only specific employees can make requests to the marketing department, and all requests must be run through the marketing director first. This prevents Joe in sales from asking for a last-minute social post from Peggy the copywriter.
  - Designate a budgeted quantity of marketing hours allowed for each department. This turns the internal marketing department into a budgeted and *limited* resource. If no budget is in place, then it is an unlimited resource that can become very expensive.
  - Require a business case to be provided for every request of the marketing department. This assures that every task has the proper thought behind it. All too often marketing teams react to new ideas that are not well thought out and never come to fruition.

Three: Hold Regular Marketing Meetings

Regular weekly or monthly meetings are the best way to bring deliverables and action items to light on time. Let's face it, the biggest issues are poor planning and communication.

Regular marketing team meetings also keep everyone in alignment and accountable. Talk about internal and external support needs and have an agenda to ensure the meeting has a purpose and goal, not just meeting for the sake of meeting. That's a time-waster.

Conclusion

Evaluating your company's marketing needs to achieve better marketing efficiency starts by addressing internal bandwidth and capabilities gaps. Defining clear roles and rules can enable meeting internal needs while still supporting strategic external initiatives. Then, holding regular stakeholder meetings further optimizes operations. Taking these steps will allow your organization to properly balance priorities.

U2

Chapter 2
Goal Setting to Brand Positioning

In this chapter, we help businesses determine their growth goals and desired brand positioning to help them make the most of the tactics discussed in the rest of the book.

Evaluating your company's current and future needs requires looking at growth goals and current standing versus desired brand positioning. The overarching goals of why a company engages in marketing and advertising are multifaceted and can vary depending on the company's industry, size, and stage of growth. However, there are several common objectives that most companies seek to achieve through these activities. Let's start with why you may have picked up this book, as it's likely to do with one or several of the following goals.

Generating Demand and Sales

This is the most common goal clients come to us with. They have a large sales team, and they are looking for more qualified leads. The basis of marketing to increase demand and sales is developing creative that stimulates interest in a product or service. This can be achieved by showcasing the benefits, features, and value of what the company offers.

Increasing Brand Awareness and Recognition

One of the primary goals is to increase brand awareness and recognition. Many times companies come to us with this goal after they have previously grown through acquisition and customer referrals. However, to achieve the next level of growth, they need to make more potential customers aware of the brand and its products or services. The more familiar people are with a brand, the more likely they are to consider it when making a purchase. Additionally, the more a consumer is exposed to a brand, the more they trust it, and this trust translates into a higher likelihood of choosing that brand over competitors.

Building and Maintaining Customer Relationships

Companies use marketing to build and maintain relationships with their customers. Building relationships is much like farming. The more you put into growing your crops, the more they produce. The same goes for customer relationships—the more you build strong customer relationships, the more revenue they will produce.

That revenue typically comes through increased customer lifespan and the purchase of additional products and services. Engaging with your customers and understanding their needs and preferences allows you to provide more products and services to them. You can also encourage ongoing engagement and foster loyalty among existing customers through loyalty programs and regular communication that provides exceptional customer experiences.

Brand Positioning

Establishing or altering the market position of the company or its products is key to your marketing strategy. This involves differentiating the brand from competitors and positioning it in a way that appeals to the target market. We will expand on this later in the chapter.

Educating Customers

Informing and educating potential and existing customers about products and services is crucial. Clients that have innovative and market-disruptive technology often come to us with this goal. This education can include how to use a product, its benefits, the solutions it offers, or updates and improvements.

Supporting Business Growth and Market Expansion

We use the word "growth" because almost zero companies desire to stay the same size or decline in size. Growth could mean a couple of different things but should be defined geographically and demographically for your marketing efforts.

Geographics and demographics can overlap. Demographically, we're referring to a person's behaviors, interests, age, sex, income, and so forth. Geographics refers to a location. However, I might target someone differently in Miami than in San Diego or New York City. Understanding these geographies is integral to marketing success.

Let's illustrate three typical ways companies achieve their growth goals utilizing a New York City general contractor as the example company:

- **Market expansion into a new demographic:** A New York City general contractor wants to sell more of the same services in the same region but to a more upscale and wealthier demographic.

- **Market expansion into a new geographic:** A New York City general contractor would like to open new locations in Miami and Chicago, and provide the same services that have brought them great success in their original location.

- **Market expansion of new products and services:** A New York City general contractor would like to now provide solar energy solutions to the same demographic in the same geography.

Company Goals Drive Marketing Strategy

Without a clear understanding of your company's goals, it will be impossible to align a marketing strategy. This means your company's leadership is integral to your marketing success. Best practices call for quarterly leadership meetings to measure and discuss how the above data and goals have evolved or changed. Tracking of company KPIs (e.g., revenue by state, overall products sold, contact form submissions, etc.) will also be integral to measuring marketing success and ROI.

Business leadership will need to provide answers to the following questions so that you can align your marketing strategy:

- What demographics represent most of your revenue?

- What current or new demographics would you like to have more growth in?

- What regions (e.g., countries, cities, states) represent most of your revenue?

- What current or new regions (if any) would you like to grow in?

- What is the revenue by service in order of most to least?

- What products/services have the largest opportunity to grow?

- Conversely, are there products/services that you expect to phase out?

- How is your brand currently positioned? And does that need to change to support the above initiatives?

Positioning and Branding Goals

Brand positioning is how your audience sees your company, how they identify with it, and how your company can solve their problems, needs, and wants. To create your desired brand positioning, you will require a deliberate strategy of how your brand looks, what it says, how it says it, and where it is said.

Your positioning may change as you launch new campaigns or as your company grows. For example, a company launching a new product or service may require updated positioning to generate awareness and better resonate with a desired target audience, but their overall identity will remain the same throughout the campaign.

We once worked with a client whose sales team numbered in the hundreds. Their main business was leasing and selling copy machines. However, they recognized that it was a dying industry and were eager to redefine themselves as the go-to tech provider for companies.

Their work had gone well beyond copy machines for years. They were actively involved in offering VoIP telephone installations, providing IT support, and managing other essential technical parts of an office environment. So, getting a solid grasp on their business growth goals was crucial and helped guide decisions regarding the strategy we needed to develop.

An outdated company is a prime example of the need for revised positioning and/or brand strategy. And it's common for our agency to assist and lead those repositioning efforts.

A national wholesale distributor of electrical supplies came to us because their brand was out of date. The company is family owned with the fourth generation running the business. The company still supplies the same product to the same types of buyers that it had for decades but has grown in size over time. The brand was ancient, with the same logo since the early 1900s. It was not well defined—the blue and gold colors in the logo lacked definition, as did the fonts and messaging. Two different taglines were associated with the brand—so evolving the brand was paramount. We kept some of their primary colors and added tertiary colors to refresh the brand while evolving their tagline and updating sub-messaging to relate to the services they still provide. Ensuring they still looked relevant in an increasingly competitive marketplace was vital.

Repositioning Our Company's Brand

Let me conclude this chapter by sharing a story about my company's branding.

I designed our logo in 2004 when I started the company. After a few years, people told me it looked outdated. I took exception. Their opinions seemed unnecessary, like they didn't know what they were talking about. Many also thought The Kraus Group (Kraus Marketing's original name) was a law firm or accounting company. I ignored that conversation many times because, to me, changing it was personal.

However, I took a step back and, through the convincing of my team and others, realized it was time to make that change. If people needed to learn what we did by the name, changing it from The Kraus Group to Kraus Marketing might be essential. It was important for my name to be on it. (Perhaps that was selfish, but that is a story for another time.)

Positioning and branding are a matter of perception. The fact is, perception is reality, and you must accept that. Most people saw The Kraus Group branding as older, stodgy, irrelevant, or unrelatable to my industry, necessitating a brand name, logo, and messaging change.

An unbiased review of your growth, positioning, and branding strategy is essential because you need to know how your company is perceived to grow successfully. Having your brand and positioning solidified helps ensure that all the tactics and platforms we will discuss later are well aligned and give customers and prospects the perception that your company is the best option.

To determine if you have the correct brand positioning, you can ask a series of strategic questions that delve into the effectiveness of your positioning strategy, its alignment with your target audience, and its differentiation from competitors.

Here are some key questions to consider when evaluating your current brand positioning:

1. **Does your positioning align with your target audience?**

   - Who is your target audience, and what are their needs, preferences, and behaviors?

   - Does your brand positioning resonate with this audience?

   - How does your target audience perceive your brand?

2. **Is your unique selling proposition (USP) clear and compelling?**

   - What is your brand's USP?

   - Is it clearly communicated in your marketing messages?

   - Do your customers understand and value your USP?

3. How does your brand compare to competitors?

- Who are your main competitors, and how are they positioned?
- What makes your brand different from these competitors?
- Is this differentiation important to your target audience?

4. Is your brand positioning consistent across all channels?

- Are you consistently conveying your brand positioning across all marketing channels (e.g., website, social media, advertising platforms)?
- Do all elements of your brand (logo, messaging, tone) reflect your intended positioning?

5. Are customers responding positively to your positioning?

- How are customers reacting to your brand?
- Are you seeing engagement, loyalty, and advocacy?
- Is there feedback or data that suggests your positioning is effective?

6. Does your positioning support your business goals?

- How does your brand positioning contribute to your overall business objectives?
- Are you attracting the right customers and achieving your sales and marketing goals?

7. **Is your positioning adaptable and future proof?**

- Is your brand positioning flexible enough to adapt to market changes?
- How does it position your company for future growth and opportunities?

8. **What insights do market research and data provide?**

- What does market research say about your brand's position in the market?
- Are there data-driven insights (from sales data, customer feedback, and market analysis) that support or challenge your positioning?

By answering these questions, you can evaluate the effectiveness of your current brand positioning and identify areas that may need refinement or adjustment. It's important to remember that brand positioning is not static; it should evolve with your business, market trends, and customer preferences.

Conclusion

Determining growth objectives and desired brand positioning is essential to aligning marketing strategies. Business leaders must clearly convey target demographics, geographic focus, product mix, and branding goals. With this vision, marketers can shape data-driven campaigns tailored to meet organizational aims.

U3

Chapter 3
Develop the Creative Brief

**This chapter aims to help marketers understand
what a creative brief is, its importance, and how
to develop one for use in a marketing campaign.**

What Is a Creative Brief (and Why Do I Need One?)

A creative brief is a marketing campaign playbook that includes the company's vision, growth goals, brand position, and campaign purpose. Think of it like a "constitution" to which you align your campaign goals and objectives or as a compass that keeps you on course.

The creative brief is a living document. It can be changed as your brand objectives evolve, but the goal is to have a brief that your team can constantly refer to. It details the campaign objectives, target audience, voice, mission statement, and other essential elements.

The creative brief helps align teams, whether in-house, freelancers, agencies, or all the above. It lets designers, developers, writers, strategists, and even the C-suite know where you are and where you want to go.

Creative briefs can be as detailed or as streamlined as you like. We've seen briefs for smaller companies be as few as two pages. Larger companies may create fifty-page PowerPoint decks. The number of elements you include dictates the length. Typically, the bigger the company, the longer the brief because there are more elements.

What a Creative Brief Should Include

Company Background

The company background is a brief history of the company. If you're going to understand the brand, you need to reference the company's history: how it started, how it has evolved, and where leadership wants to take it. The background can also include the company's main services and mission statement, vision statement, and value proposition.

Brand Identity Guidelines

Brand identity guidelines include all the visual elements, such as the company logo (how it's scaled, where it's used, and color options), color palettes, and typography (including when to use a particular font, such as online or print).

Campaign Objective

This area includes growth and brand positioning goals. What is your company looking to achieve through your marketing initiatives? Have you increased brand recognition or revenue? A higher following on social media or visits to your storefront? Without setting clear goals, you leave your campaigns open to misdirection.

Target Audience

We won't know where to aim if we don't have a target. We define a target audience in detail below, but first let's explain what a target audience is *not*—and that's "everyone."

For example, we hear many clients say, "My target audience is anyone who needs a real estate lawyer." But you, as a real estate lawyer, may not be able to handle a $100 million project, or you may be able to manage a $1 billion project and not want a $400,000 house sale. So, as you can see, having a detailed target audience is extremely important.

The best way to develop a target audience is to focus on your company's growth and brand positioning goals. Consider your best customers and be specific: "John Doe, CEO of XYZ Company, is my best customer." Develop your target audience around that persona.

There is often more than one target audience at any company. Once you finish defining one, typically, you must specify a couple of others to cover all major audience groups. At Kraus Marketing, we take our clients through a comprehensive workshop to help them develop their target audiences. This often lasts for several hours and includes key players from the company in question, including C-suite members, decision-makers, and sales team members.

For each audience, we define demographics (e.g., name, title, location, income, and personality traits), backstory and pain points, current needs, and how to exceed their requirements. Once we gather this information, we summarize it for inclusion in the brief.

Voice

Your company voice is the target audience's perception of how your brand sounds in your marketing materials: online, in print, and in person. You want your brand voice to be cohesive because you want your brand to be cohesive. Don't sound pushy in your ads and then welcoming on your website. Keep the voice and tone uniform across all channels.

Conversion Goals

What do you want the audience to do after interacting with your campaign? Whether it's making a purchase, filling out a quote form, signing up for a newsletter, or visiting a website, be specific about the desired action.

General Dos and Don'ts

This part is essential, especially for companies that deal with legal regulations. Depending on the industry, there are many things that companies can say and things they cannot. Having a running list as part of the creative brief that stakeholders can access makes your campaign more efficient and prevents hurdles.

For example, a general contracting company's rule would be not to have anyone featured in a picture that isn't wearing branded clothing or the proper safety harnesses or hats. The financial industry is very compliance focused, so an investment company cannot say they guarantee clients will make money. General dos and don'ts prevent common mistakes that can lead to more complex issues.

Competitive Analysis

There are two reasons to include a competitive analysis: One, you want your brand to look unique, not like you're copying a competitor. Two, it helps you leverage what marketing tactics work in the industry because, many times, similar tactics will work for companies within the same vertical.

Competitive analyses also help you get a baseline knowledge of where to start if you're unsure and can help you better understand your brand's audience when you see who your competitors attract. You can better wrap your head around your brand when you know how it contrasts with others.

Desired KPIs

What specific metrics will determine the success of the campaign? Examples include website traffic, conversion rates, social media engagement, or sales figures. In chapter 10 we outline key KPIs for specific types of campaigns.

Conclusion

The creative brief serves as the guidelines for your brand strategy. A great brief should include all information and links to information that your team of creatives (designers, copywriters, and producers) needs to make sure their work aligns with the brand and campaign(s). Once your team has parameters, it's time to set a plan.

U4

Chapter 4
The Importance of a
Content Calendar

This chapter focuses on the importance of
creative and campaign messaging, how to
develop a successful campaign, and strategies
for determining the right audience fit.

The success of any marketing campaign hinges on one critical factor: a well-designed, strategic content calendar. If we don't have good creative and good content, the other tactics will be completely useless.

The content calendar is essential to developing an overarching marketing strategy that clears the path for how things look in the year ahead. It also increases efficiency and streamlines content ideation, often a time-consuming process. It serves as a single source of truth that aligns all organizational stakeholders, regardless of their department or role, ensuring everyone is on the same page and working toward the same goals.

Perhaps the most important aspect of the content calendar is its flexibility. It's not etched in stone but can adapt to changing circumstances. Although it may change, the strategy is to put something in place based on the business's goals and forecast for the entire year.

Content Calendar Defined

When we refer to a content calendar, we're talking about an editorial calendar, similar to what magazine publishers use. However, their calendars only relate to the articles they will print over the next twelve months. Our calendar is the roadmap for all the deliverables we produce for the entire year: visual, text, audio, and otherwise. It expands on the creative brief we discussed in chapter 3 and delves into the actual strategy we use to create the content.

In the early 2000s, I worked with companies doing earned media (i.e., public relations). I learned that everything hinged on the editorial calendar if you create content for a particular digital or print publication. If you pitched them on calendar-related content, you had a better chance of getting into that week's or month's edition.

I looked at these editorial calendars and thought, "What great tools for them to know what they will write about all year." It allows them to sync up internally and enables other marketers, like PR companies, to pitch them on the topic and create content to include in the publication.

Then I thought about our marketing strategy and how a calendar like this would benefit us since we have so many departments working on each campaign. Understanding the concept and then reverse engineering how they put it together was the start of our content calendar and how we set it up. Think of it like a waterfall—it starts big and flows down to the details.

Content Calendars and Customer Personas

The first step in developing a content calendar is to focus on your clients' or customers' cyclical buying habits.

What happens throughout the year in your company, and how do those things change? Most companies we work with—B2B, B2C, or D2C—are seasonal regarding their products and services.

Take a hospitality company, for example. Let's say a hotel in a tropical location. If that hotel thinks about its customers, they could fall into three personas: The Planner, The Improvisor, and Future Guests. These seasonal buying behaviors relate to the content and creative elements we will develop. Here's how that would start to break down based on these cyclical buying behaviors we identified.

The Planner. These customers plan well in advance of their trip, at least three months to a year. For that reason, the offseason is a great time to educate consumers, inspire interest, and plan advanced promotions. Schedule seasonal marketing to start during the fall or winter when people plan a spring or summer trip as much as a year in advance.

The Improvisor. The last-minute people are more like me. Marketing efforts for last-minute purchases would begin just before the season starts. It's less than three months until our paid time off, but we haven't planned our vacation yet. Last-minute purchases require heavy calls to action and promotional content: "why you should plan that trip now" type of content and creative.

Future Guests. In-season purchasing will be slower, but that doesn't mean the hotel should give up on its marketing. This is an ideal time to create FOMO (fear of missing out) promotions for those who didn't get their plans together earlier. Showing the amazing experiences that people are having creates demand for future seasons.

Let's talk about a completely different type of business: accounting firms. They, too, are seasonal. They have two extremely busy times per year: fall, when they do corporate tax returns, and spring, when they do personal returns.

Many accounting firms give up on marketing during these times. However, we find that we get the target audience's attention during those busiest times because they are focused on accounting services.

If I were the owner of an accounting firm, I would break down the year into four distinct cycles: spring and fall, which are the busiest times, and the remaining two cycles, summer and winter, which are slower periods when we aren't primarily focused on tax preparation. To make our content strategy more effective, I would tailor it to address specific pain points during the busy seasons and prioritize educational and thought leadership content during the slower periods.

How to Develop a Content Calendar

Once we understand the seasonality of a customer's buying journey, we can break our marketing down month-by-month, creating a twelve-month calendar with each month's theme.

Let's say my customer is in a particular place in the buying journey from January through March. I develop relevant themes and serve content at just the right time for that part of their journey. Themes could be educational or technical; they could elicit desire or emotion for the products or services offered, but each could contain different types of content and different ways to present it.

For the hotel brand, content may relate to guests' experiences, such as adventures, leisure, food, and other areas of interest. An accounting firm would likely include taxes, financial planning, and business advice in its content mix.

Regarding the various content types, we often start with long-form, such as blog posts. We create more short-form content from there, like YouTube videos and social media posts. We may also create a webinar campaign for the accounting firm, accompanied by pay-per-click ads and email blasts.

A blog post for the hotel might be about ten things to do in Cancun. You can link to the blog from social media posts highlighting each activity. An example might be that 75 percent of people who go to Cancun say that snorkeling is their favorite activity. Or you could produce a six-minute video about snorkeling in Cancun, then cut it down to fifteen seconds for use as an Instagram Story.

For example, a January theme for Kraus Marketing could be "Plan your annual digital marketing strategy." Our blogs, videos, and social posts relate to that theme. February's theme might be "Websites," and March might be "Social Media." We try to focus on topics people think about at different times of the year. From there we create content based on those topics.

The process so far is to (1) understand the customer's buying habits and the business's seasonal cycles, (2) develop a twelve-month content calendar tied to the creative brief, utilizing themes that relate to the customer journey, and (3) build out relevant topics and content types.

Let's venture further down the waterfall and discuss content topics and placement.

Deciding on Content Topics

How do you decide what content topics to choose? It goes back to the creative brief, the target audience, and their pain points. Another way is to research issues on Google that the industry and competition are publishing, then customize those to your brand and content calendar.

Pro tip: AI has sped up this process. You can request it to provide a list of topics related to your theme and then cherry-pick the ones that match your creative brief goals.

It's worth noting that every piece of content does not have to relate to a theme. There is also a need for thought leadership content that applies to the company's unique opinion, analysis, or evolution of services and products. It's less timely but rounds out who you are as a company and increases your brand value.

You must also create content based on your target audience's interests, needs, and pain points.

Take automobile manufacturers, for example. The way Jeep talks about its cars during the winter season may be different from Volvo's approach. Volvo may talk about the vehicle's safety during wintertime driving, while Jeep might describe all the exciting places you can visit. The two brands' target audiences are not alike; they care about different things.

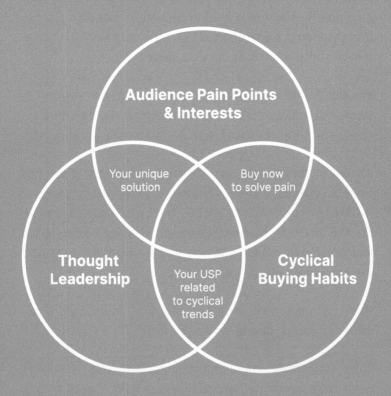

Utilizing this Venn diagram can help with core topic ideation, ensuring you focus on the interests, pain points, and buying habits of your target audience.

Determining Content Placement

Where you publish content is also part of the waterfall. Once we have the twelve-month calendar with themed content, we move on to the next step: breaking the content into specific tactics and channels.

How can we utilize it within social media? What keywords can we create that people will search for, whether paid or organic? What webinars can we put together around them? What videos can we make? Regardless of the type, everything we create falls within *The Sharkbite Method*™. It will be part of the website, social media, search, email, or media buying tactic.

- **Company website.** The content calendar should include improvements to the website, such as adding to your services, blog, or news section.

- **Search engine marketing.** When creating the content calendar, consider the keywords people search for in any monthly theme. That practice will help you create long-form blog posts, pay-per-click campaign ads, and landing pages.

- **Social media.** Create posts and videos that include links to the long-form content on your website.

- **Email.** Insert the source content into email drip and promotional campaigns.

- **Media buys.** The content calendar and theme should influence the creative within media buys.

Creating multiple touch points utilizing the above tactics will make your brand memorable for its target audience.

By placing your brand messages cross-channel, the odds of them seeing it repeatedly increase. Increasing those odds increases the odds of conversion because, typically, no one will purchase an item or service they only saw once.

A Strategic Plan

The content calendar holds immense strategic importance in your marketing efforts. By prioritizing creative and campaign messaging as the first step in your process, you set the stage for success. By understanding your target audience's preferences, aligning your content with cyclical and seasonal buying habits, breaking down themes into specific content topics and types, and ensuring cross-channel placement, you can deliver impactful and memorable campaigns that resonate with your audience, resulting in earning a bigger ROI for the company in the most efficient manner possible.

Conclusion

A strategic content calendar aligns marketing campaigns for resonance and memorability. By planning creative concepts tuned to seasonal purchase cycles and distributing across targeted channels, brands convey the right messages at the optimal times to compel their audiences.

Quick Start Guide

Create an annual content calendar in two easy steps:

1. **Create four quarterly themes based on cyclical industry trends and buying behaviors.**

2. **Create three topics within each quarterly theme.**

Q1

- _____
- _____
- _____

Q2

- _____
- _____
- _____

Q3

- _____
- _____
- _____

Q4

- _____
- _____
- _____

Next, build out your content calendar in full, one to three months in advance, utilizing the waterfall chart below:

1. **Create a list of blog posts for each month. Each post should have a focused keyword.**

2. **Utilize social media and email to distribute this thought leadership content.**

3. **Get creative and use videos, infographics, and media to support monthly themes.**

Cyclical Buying Habits	Month	Blog Articles	Keywords	Email	Videos/ Infographics	Social Media
Winter Buying Habit 1	January Theme	Topic 1	Focus Keyword For Topic			Organic Post: Topic 1
		Topic 2	Focus Keyword For Topic	Email 1	Video: Topic 2	Organic Post: Topic 2
		Topic 3	Focus Keyword For Topic			Organic Post: Topic 3
		Topic 4	Focus Keyword For Topic	Email 2	Infographic: Topic 4	Organic Post: Topic 4
						Paid Ad: Topic 2
						Paid Ad: Topic 4
	February Theme	Topic 1	Focus Keyword For Topic			Organic Post: Topic 1
		Topic 2	Focus Keyword For Topic	Email 1	Video: Topic 2	Organic Post: Topic 2
		Topic 3	Focus Keyword For Topic			Organic Post: Topic 3
		Topic 4	Focus Keyword For Topic	Email 2	Infographic: Topic 4	Organic Post: Topic 4
						Paid Ad: Topic 2
						Paid Ad: Topic 4

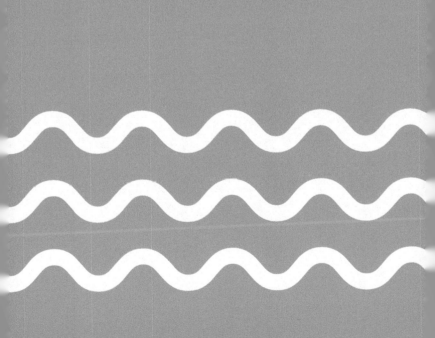

Part II
The Sharkbite Method™: Strategy Execution

The Sharkbite Method™ marketing strategies and tactics we use and recommend.

U5

Chapter 5
Optimize Your Website to Increase Conversions

This chapter's goal is to drive home the point that the brand website is the epicenter of all digital marketing activities and should be optimized to achieve the best results.

Imagine pouring water into a leaky bucket. No matter how much water (or marketing budget) you pour, you'll lose a significant amount due to the leaks (poor website conversion). Conversion optimization works to seal those leaky holes, ensuring every drop you pour in (each digital campaign) remains effective and gives you the fullest return. Without working to seal the bucket, you're simply wasting water, no matter how high quality or plentiful it may be.

Your brand website is the hub of all your digital marketing activities. Therefore, optimizing the user experience (UX) and user interface (UI) to achieve the best results is essential. Let me share a couple of stories that illustrate the importance of website optimization and how it can significantly impact your business.

Website Optimization: An E-commerce Consumer Products Website

Early in my business, I was approached by the owner of a small luxury items resale company that faced some challenges. The client had created a marketplace for buying consignment bags, a relatively new concept at the time. They successfully sold luxury bags on eBay, but once they reached a certain monthly sales volume, their page and account would shut down.

Despite making tens of thousands of dollars in sales on eBay, they had never once made a sale on their website—and that was after spending a lot of time and money working with a developer to create a website that had all the features you would expect to find in an e-commerce store.

The owner came to us frustrated and confused but highly motivated to find a solution. We determined there had to be a UX and/or UI issue but wouldn't know for sure until we examined the site further.

Several issues surfaced once we looked at the site, but one stood out: the site lacked authenticity and trustworthiness. It gave off a low-end, generic vibe and poor user experience. There was no real brand identity, just a templated site with poor quality images of nice bags. Therefore, it lacked the high-end design and user interface quality the consumer of luxury handbags is accustomed too.

During the UX audit, we outlined the following:

Font: The website lacked consistent use of font type, size, weight, and color. Consciously or subconsciously, most consumers will not trust a brand that does not use consistent typography. The reason is that it appears unorganized, amateurish, and unattractive.

Color scheme: The color scheme lacked a high-end feel. Hot pink ran through the site, making it seem monotone. Color has been used for thousands of years to denote wealth and hierarchy. For instance, in ancient Rome, purple was associated with royalty and the elite because the dye used to produce this color was very expensive and rare. It came from the *Murex* sea snail and took thousands of these snails to produce just a small amount of dye. This made purple cloth prohibitively expensive and it thus became a symbol of wealth, power, and status. For that reason, we chose to move away from the hot pink and change her color palette to contain accents of purple and gold, another universally recognized symbol of wealth, as these better matched the high-end products she was selling.

Imagery: The imagery was also inconsistent; some were even blurry. Product backgrounds varied, reducing the user experience, making it difficult for customers to understand what they were purchasing. Product pages also had missing details.

A business website should never contain blurry images and stock photography, a mantra that applies to consumer products and service companies alike. That's why we always believe in using professional headshots or product photography, video testimonials, and clear calls to action. Good imagery is essential to website optimization and conversions.

When a consumer purchases a product online, the seller must sit back and understand what someone needs to know to complete the sale. Visually, the answer is a 360-degree view of the product and its dimensions, specs, and benefits.

That meant we needed to create guidelines for how her products should be photographed (and how they shouldn't) and create additional fields in the products' long description that included dimensions, age, condition, color, and other factors.

In the end, we completely redesigned the website and e-commerce platform, utilizing an adaptable and customizable content management system (CMS). The results were nothing less than remarkable. Within the first six months of launching the new site, sales skyrocketed from zero to over $1.2 million.

To say the owner was relieved would be an understatement. She was elated over the results, happy and confident in her new site and brand. Since the redesign, the company continued to grow online. She also developed a multi-location brick-and-mortar presence in most major U.S. markets, eventually selling the business for a tidy sum.

Website Optimization for a B2B Company

In another case, we worked with a last-minute shipping and LTL (less-than-truckload) company struggling to generate leads and conversions through their website. Despite having decent traffic and years of SEO efforts, they were not receiving many quote requests or calls for their trucks. Most of their business came from referrals and loyal customers.

The owner had taken over the business from his father, who had died suddenly of a heart attack. It took a few years, but he finally got the company back to where it was before his father passed. He knew he had many challenges, so he came to us to update his digital presence and improve his website.

We analyzed the site and discovered a lack of compelling calls to action (CTAs), live chat support, and an easy-to-use quote form. These are critical for converting visitors, particularly in this industry.

First, we created larger and more noticeable CTAs to guide visitors toward taking action.

A call to action is necessary because it tells the person what you want them to do next. Calls to action are typically higher in contrast and have larger font sizes than the rest of the content, drawing the user's eyes to the text. The copy gives them the next steps. Examples of standard CTAs you find on websites include "Learn more," "Click here to download," "Fill out the quote form," or "Add to cart."

We also added a live chat feature, allowing people who preferred not to make phone calls or wait on hold to engage in a real-time chat with a customer representative. In this case, an actual person managed the chat, but the plan is to eventually evolve to use an AI-powered chatbot.

Many people think implementing a chatbot is hard; however, most don't understand the efficiency it can create. The advantage of a chatbot is that it can be open 24-7, allowing people to communicate with the company at their convenience. Also, the chatbot's ability to answer consumers' questions by utilizing a series of pathways replaces the need for a customer support representative, reducing company overhead.

Lastly, we developed a user-friendly quote form that enabled visitors to receive accurate quotes directly on the website. Quote forms give a consumer a sense of efficiency and instant gratification when receiving an estimate or the next step immediately upon completion.

The results were astounding. The conversion rate improved from 0.7% to 2%. Although a 1.3% increase may seem small, it translated into a 300% overall conversion improvement. It generated millions of dollars in additional revenue for the company, outcomes that changed the man's business (and life), allowing him to scale and produce more profit. These remarkable results also proved the website's ROI value, so much so that we continue to work with him today. His company has been a client for almost a decade.

These stories demonstrate the power of website optimization. The first example showcased the importance of a complete website redesign to align with the brand and products sold, ultimately creating a business that consumers could love and trust. The second highlighted the value of incremental improvements in conversion optimization, which can lead to significant financial gains and efficiencies for your business.

By focusing on your website and ensuring it effectively represents your brand, incorporates compelling CTAs, provides convenient communication options like live chat, and offers user-friendly forms, you can drive conversions and boost revenue. Remember, every incremental improvement counts. Even seemingly minor changes can make a substantial difference in your top and (more importantly) bottom line.

The Crucial Importance of Website Optimization

As the saying goes, people judge a book by its cover. In the digital age, the same principle applies: people judge a company by its website. To drive conversions, whether a sale or quote request, you need a fantastic website that accurately reflects your brand and instills visitor trust.

Website optimization is essential for several other reasons. It allows your site to communicate directly with your target audience. Unlike printed materials, websites are digital and, for that reason, easy to update. Your company's services and products may evolve with your customers' changing needs. It's crucial to update your website to reflect these changes and ensure it effectively showcases how your company can address your customers' challenges.

Moreover, website optimization is vital because you invest significant resources in driving site traffic through your marketing efforts. Your website must accurately represent your products and services to maximize the return on this investment. For example, a paid social media campaign wastes funds if your posts lead to a website that turns away visitors.

Website Optimization—Getting Started

What do we mean by website optimization? The previous examples illustrate the meaning, but let's delve deeper into what optimization entails and how to go about it.

Start with a website audit. Assess your website's current state and document its strengths and weaknesses.

- **Is your website up to date?** Outdated content can give a negative impression to visitors.

- **Does your website effectively communicate with your target audience?** You must ensure that your messaging aligns with their pain points and needs.

- **Are your services/products accurately represented on your website?** Remove outdated services/products and include new offerings.

- **Do you highlight the industries you serve?** This helps potential customers understand your expertise and clarify your offerings.

- **Do you have a company culture or about us page?** These pages help customers and prospects learn more about your company, its culture, history, and leadership. It can help bring a human element to your brand that prospects may seek.

- **Do you have a blog or news section?** If so, is it informative and engaging? Regularly updating your blog with substantive content boosts SEO value and enhances your website's credibility and thought leadership.

- **Is your site easy to navigate?** A clear and intuitive navigation structure improves the user experience.

- **If service related, are there lead-generation tools like live chat and contact forms?** Make it easy for visitors to engage with you and convert.

- **If e-commerce, is purchasing your products easy?** Make it easy for visitors to purchase, repurchase, and sign up for special offers.

- **Is your website optimized for mobile devices?** Mobile responsiveness is essential for reaching a wider audience and converting leads from mobile users.

This assessment forms the foundation for improving your website and optimizing it for conversion. In chapter 10, we highlight the main KPIs and their benchmarks to make it easy to identify where your website is falling short.

Once you clearly understand your website's performance, you can leverage the insights gained from the assessment. Consider whether your site effectively presents your company's products and services and whether it addresses your target audience's pain points and challenges. These questions guide the optimization process and help you determine the necessary steps. An easy-to-use CMS is crucial for optimizing and implementing the actions that follow without encountering too many hurdles.

Conversion Optimization

Let's address the concept of conversion optimization, a crucial part of website optimization.

Conversion optimization ensures that your site effectively converts visitors into taking specific actions. It's essential to clarify that conversion is the action you want the user to take rather than something they happen to do while scrolling around your website.

The desired action is different for every company. For a B2B company, a conversion might be a user who fills out a quote form, calls your company, or submits an RFP (request for proposal). Conversely, a conversion for a B2C company could be making a sale directly on the website. A conversion could also be as simple as getting visitors to subscribe to your newsletter or view a specific landing page to build awareness around a new product or service. A conversion that relates directly to revenue isn't always required. It's about the goals you need your website to meet for your business.

Conversion examples include (but are not limited to):
- Contact/Quote/RFP form submissions
- E-commerce sales
- Email/Newsletter signups
- Marketing material downloads (e.g., sell sheet or eBook)
- Landing page visits
- Video plays

The Power of Heat Mapping

To optimize conversions, we utilize a tactic called heat mapping. Several online services offer heat mapping software, but we currently use Crazy Egg (www.crazyegg. com).

Heat mapping overlays your website and provides insights into how users interact with the pages. It reveals how far users scroll, where they click, if users appear frustrated by your UX, and more. You can even capture anonymous screen recordings of a user's experience on your site, revealing load times, how fast they scroll, if they jump to another page, or if they perform other actions. We can make informed decisions to improve the user experience by analyzing this data. The information it provides is revealing.

Often, you think people will scroll more than they do or won't scroll as much as they will. It's the same with clicks. Sometimes, people click on what they think are buttons and links but aren't, and overlook those that are! You may never be able to see this without heat mapping.

Image 5.1 Heat Map Scrolling: This image illustrates how users scroll and view your page. The warmer colors (red, orange, yellow) indicate where the users spend the most time viewing. The cooler colors (green, blue, purple) indicate where the users spend the least amount of time.

Image 5.2 Heat Map Clicks: This image illustrates where users click within your website interface. The warmer click area (red, orange, yellow) indicates where people are clicking the most. The cooler colors (green, blue, purple) indicate fewer clicks.

You should collect heat mapping data from a significant number of users, preferably several hundred or even several thousand. A sufficient data sample ensures reliable insights for optimization; otherwise, it wastes time. In some circumstances—depending on your company's reach, timeframe, and goals—a couple of weeks is enough; for others, two to three months is required.

You can make various changes based on the heat mapping results, such as rearranging content hierarchy to prioritize important information and calls to action. You may want to redesign buttons, update link colors, resize images, and cut or add sections. A UX/UI designer can interpret the heat mapping data for more in-depth optimization and implement best practices to enhance user experience.

We use a tool called Google Optimize to take it a step further. This allows marketers to create an A/B test that will serve up two versions of a page, allowing you to analyze and measure which version performs better. This way you won't spend too much time guessing.

Website Optimization for Mobile Devices

Mobile device optimization is yet another critical aspect of website optimization you must consider. Conversions on mobile devices may differ from those on desktops, so paying attention to how users interact with your website across various devices, including smartphones, tablets, and laptop and desktop computers is necessary. You can use Google Analytics to identify the technology your visitors employ to access your website. Its data will help you determine where to focus your optimization efforts.

Load times play a crucial role in mobile optimization, as users expect fast-loading pages with improvements in cellular bandwidth. Optimizing mobile screens' user interface by removing unnecessary content can enhance the mobile experience.

It's important to note that separate mobile websites are no longer the norm. Instead, responsive websites that adapt to different screen and browser sizes are preferred. However, additional coding may be required to ensure a seamless mobile experience. This may involve optimizing load times, reducing content displayed on smaller screens, and creating a mobile-friendly UI.

Website Optimization Best Practices

When it comes to website optimization, keep these best practices in mind:

- Easy-to-use site navigation is a top priority. It ensures users can traverse your website effortlessly. Regarding mobile sites, how you design your menu is super important. Do your research and find a style and function that works best with your content and target audience.

- Create strong and compelling CTAs to guide users toward desired conversion actions.

- Implement an ongoing plan to keep your website current and relevant, whether that be weekly, monthly, or quarterly.

- Redesign your website every two to four years to align it with your evolving brand.

- Regularly update imagery and video content to avoid outdated visuals that can negatively impact your brand in the visitors' minds.

- Opt for an easy-to-use CMS that allows your internal team and external vendors to manage and update your website effectively. WordPress and HubSpot are two popular options, but many others exist. We recommend avoiding using a proprietary CMS, as it usually eliminates or limits the ability to switch to a new marketing or website vendor.

Conclusion

As a company's digital portal, an optimized website shapes first impressions and enables direct communication. Enhanced performance through incremental improvements or redesigns impacts visibility, credibility, leads, and revenue. From aesthetics to mobile readiness, every aspect works in harmony to achieve marketing goals.

By implementing these best practices and continuously optimizing your website, you can create a powerful user experience that drives conversions and delivers exceptional user experiences.

U6

Chapter 6
Drive Visibility and Growth through Search Engine Marketing

Search engine marketing (SEM) is crucial in building effective digital marketing campaigns and strategies. In this chapter, we examine organic and paid SEM and discuss how it impacts businesses in terms of visibility and customer acquisition.

Whether you operate in the B2C, B2B, or D2C space, locally, regionally, or nationally, your prospective customers are likely searching for your products and services online via a search engine. It's commonly understood in the marketing industry that the vast majority of purchases involve consulting a search engine before deciding.

With that in mind, we will explore the significance of search engine visibility and the two primary approaches: organic (search engine optimization, or SEO) and paid (pay-per-click, or PPC).

Paid vs. Organic Search Results

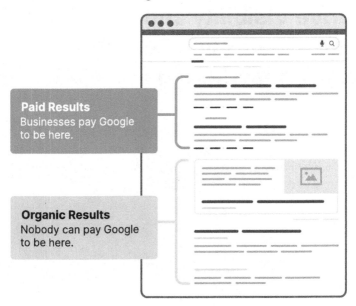

Paid Results
Businesses pay Google to be here.

Organic Results
Nobody can pay Google to be here.

Paid search results usually appear above the organic results with a label of "Sponsored" to identify it as a paid advertisement.

Paid search and organic search are two distinct approaches to driving traffic to a website through search engines. Paid search entails paying for advertising placements within search engine results pages (SERPs), guaranteeing immediate visibility at the top for specific keywords. However, it comes at a cost, and traffic generation stops when the advertising budget is exhausted. Advertisers have significant control over ad content, targeting, and bidding strategies.

On the other hand, organic search results are achieved without direct payments, with placement determined by search engine algorithms based on relevance and quality. While it may take time to rank well organically, it offers consistent, long-term traffic. Control over how and where your website appears in organic results is limited, but it is often perceived as more credible and trustworthy by users, as it is based on relevance rather than advertising.

The Power of Search Engines

When consumers or businesses are in the market for a product or service, they often turn to search engines like Google or Bing. Whether they are looking for a specific vendor or seeking multiple quotes, search engines have become an integral part of the purchase process.

This fact holds true for a wide range of businesses, from direct-to-consumer (D2C) websites selling items like shoes, apparel, or specialty items, to B2C enterprises like roofing companies, car dealerships, or restaurants, to B2B entities like accounting or law firms specializing in specific practice areas.

Even some of the largest brands and procurement officers rely on Google searches to find the right companies. At Kraus Marketing, we have experienced Fortune 100 companies reaching out to us for substantial deals discovered through Google searches. Our clients have enjoyed similar successes in attracting high-value projects or partnerships via search engine visibility.

As a case in point, an engineering firm we optimized a website for landed a deal to build a thousand cell phone sites for AT&T due to a Google search. Uber also found them while soliciting vendors for a project requiring engineering help.

Organic SEM

Search Engine Optimization: Advantages and Challenges

We worked with an international shipping company spending a significant amount on paid keyword searches, approximately $15,000 to $20,000 per month. Despite their investment, their website lacked SEO relevancy. Through hard work, we helped them achieve the top-ranking position for "shipping to and from India." This accomplishment not only allowed them to save money on pay-per-click advertising but also delivered long-term value to their website.

The distinct advantage of SEO lies in precisely that: its long-term impact. Unlike paid search results that disappear once you stop investing in them, organic rankings last for an extended period.

SparkToro, a market research company, noted the following in their 2018 research (https://sparktoro.com/blog/google-ctr-in-2018-paid-organic-no-click-searches/):

> When you appear organically on the first page of Google's search for terms related to your product, you benefit from increased credibility and trust. Research indicates that many users bypass paid search results and scroll directly to organic results, perceiving them as higher quality. For every 100 searches on Google Desktop in September 2018, there were:
>
> - 65.6 clicks on an organic result
> - 3.7 clicks on a paid result
> - 34.3 no-click searches

Furthermore, organic visibility on Google's first page of results comes at no direct cost. However, it is worth noting that achieving organic rankings has become more challenging over the years due to increased competition and evolving search engine algorithms. Therefore, it often requires dedicated effort and expertise to appear on the first page of search results.

Search Engine Optimization: Principles and Best Practices

Organic search engine optimization comprises three parts: on-page, off-page, and technical.

On-Page SEO

On-page SEO refers to optimizing the content and elements on your website to improve search engine visibility.

One of the most effective ways to incorporate organic listings into your marketing strategy is by producing keyword-optimized content. This involves ensuring that your articles, news, blog posts, service pages, and other long-form content are all optimized for relevant keywords. It's crucial to align your creative calendar with your SEO strategy, using targeted keywords to improve organic rankings.

Pro tips: First and foremost, focus on high-quality, relevant content that caters to the needs and interests of your target audience. Use well-researched keywords strategically throughout your content, including in titles, headings, and meta descriptions, while avoiding keyword stuffing.

Ensure that your website has a user-friendly structure and navigation, with clear and concise URLs.

Optimize images and multimedia elements for faster loading times and incorporate internal and external links to provide valuable information and credibility to your readers.

Finally, prioritize mobile optimization, as an increasing number of users access the web via mobile devices. By implementing these on-page SEO techniques, you can enhance your website's ranking and provide a better experience for both users and search engines.

Off-Page SEO

Off-page SEO focuses on building inbound links and backlinks from external websites to your own. These links act as referrals to your website, signaling to search engines that your site is credible and valuable. The more authoritative and relevant the websites linking to yours, the greater the impact on your search engine rankings.

Pro tips: Obtain inbound links from vendor websites, industry-related publications, customer referrals or testimonials, and reputable ranking directories. These links enhance your website's authority and can positively influence your search engine rankings.

Online reputation management is vital, so monitor mentions of your brand and engage with users to maintain a positive image. Guest posting on authoritative websites can also boost your credibility and generate relevant traffic. Remember that off-page SEO is about building trust, relevance, and authority in the eyes of search engines, which, when done effectively, can significantly improve your website's rankings and online visibility.

Technical SEO

Technical SEO revolves around optimizing the technical aspects of your website to improve its performance and user experience. Key areas to focus on include site speed optimization and structured data implementation.

Google values websites that load quickly and provide a seamless user experience. Structured data, also known as schema markup, helps search engine bots understand the content and context of your website, enhancing its visibility.

Pro tips: Prioritize site speed optimization to ensure fast and user-friendly website performance.

Additionally, incorporate structured data into your website's backend coding to provide search engines with valuable information about your content.

Finally, monitor your site's performance with tools like Google Search Console and use them to identify and resolve technical SEO issues promptly.

Paid SEM

Pay-Per-Click: Advantages and Challenges

In contrast to SEO, pay-per-click, or paid search, is an advertising channel that offers immediate visibility on search engine result pages. With a sufficient budget, you can secure the number one position for any keyword relevant to your business.

Paid search campaigns provide an opportunity to direct users to specific landing pages optimized for conversions. This focused approach increases the likelihood of converting clicks into valuable leads or customers.

Additionally, paid search advertising is user friendly and allows quick adjustments and testing. The immediate results and data from these campaigns enable marketers to make informed decisions and optimize their strategies effectively.

However, paid search advertising does come with its own set of challenges. First and foremost, conversions can be expensive, depending on the competition for your chosen keywords and the industry you operate in. It is essential to carefully monitor your return on investment to ensure your advertising spend generates the desired results.

Also, unlike organic visibility, paid listings do not provide long-term value. Once you stop paying for the ads, your visibility in the paid section of search engine results stops immediately. If not managed properly, a poorly executed paid campaign can lead to a wasted marketing budget and negative ROI.

Pay-Per-Click: Principles and Best Practices

Paid search advertising is valuable when organic rankings may not be achievable due to high competition or when you want immediate visibility for specific keywords. It can also be effective for new companies, new locations, new products or services, or during website relaunches.

Pro tip: Consider the competition versus search volume when selecting keywords for paid search campaigns. Use longer-tail keywords with specific locations, industries, or questions to manage costs. This tactic can make your keywords more unique and less expensive while still targeting relevant audiences.

When evaluating what keywords to use, keep in mind that slight keyword variations can mean completely different intent. Here are two different types of keywords:

1. Informational Keywords: Customers who are looking for information about a product or service (how and why).

- Conversion Keywords: Customers who are looking to buy and willing to fill out a quote form or make an online purchase.

Additional Principles and Best Practices for Organic and Paid SEM

- **Regularly review your analytics and conversion data** to identify high-converting organic or paid keywords. That allows you to optimize your SEO efforts and allocate resources effectively.

- When new products or services emerge, **seize the opportunity to optimize your website for related keywords**. Being an early adopter can give you a competitive advantage and help you rank higher in search results. To illustrate, when cannabis became an industry where many companies could create products to sell, we created a website devoted to cannabis marketing. That was 2017. Now, Kraus Marketing ranks extremely high for a cannabis marketing agency. We used SEM to capitalize on a new industry from which we could profit.

- For organic SEO, **avoid making massive changes to your website** at once. Test and monitor the impact of individual changes to identify what drives positive or negative outcomes.

- **Monitor paid search campaigns daily** to ensure optimal performance and budget utilization.

- **Create a negative keyword list** for keywords that may be similar but have nothing to do with your products and services. This practice ensures you don't pay for irrelevant clicks.

Incorporating SEM into Your Marketing Strategy

It is essential to align your creative and content strategies with your search engine efforts to ensure a cohesive approach to your marketing. Utilize your content calendar to identify topics for search engine–optimized blog posts and paid search keywords. By integrating SEM into your overall strategy, you can capture potential customers at various stages of the buying process, from top to bottom, and enhance your brand's visibility in search engine results.

Conclusion

In this chapter, we have explored the importance of search engine visibility and the two primary approaches to achieving it: organic and paid.

Search engines play a critical role in consumers' purchasing decisions, making it imperative for businesses to invest in SEM strategies. SEO offers long-term value and credibility, while PPC advertising provides immediate visibility and targeted conversion opportunities. However, remember that both avenues require careful consideration of budget, competition, and ROI.

Quick start guide for organic search:

1. Create a list of keyword terms related to your products or services that buyers use in search engines.

2. Create an article strategy that focuses on each of the keyword terms. Then, align those articles within your creative calendar.

3. Utilize SEO tools like Yoast to make sure your metadata is structured properly.

4. Measure results.

5. Be consistent.

Quick start guide for paid search:

1. Create a list of keyword terms related to your products or services that buyers use in search engines.

2. Create the ads associated with those keywords that include calls to action.

3. Set keyword, ad group, and daily and monthly budgets to get the most out of your paid campaigns.

4. Measure results daily and eliminate keywords that do not produce engagement and conversions.

U7

Chapter 7
Leverage Social Media for Effective Digital Marketing

This chapter emphasizes the necessity of using social media for marketing. It covers selecting the right platform, highlights the difference between paid and organic posts, describes characteristics of the four most popular platforms, and lists principles and best practices to optimize your use.

Duolingo's language learning app made such a big splash on TikTok, a social media platform known for its bite-sized video content, that many marketing insiders thought the company's success was a fluke. The reality is that they had a strategic plan they worked on for almost a year before seeing the fruits of their labor.

The turning point came with its thirty-ninth video, which garnered over 3.3 million views and 700,000 likes. Their strategy was two-fold: First, they focused on entertainment, grabbing viewers' attention, and then incorporated their brand message, making the content enjoyable and informative.

Duolingo recognized that TikTok was a unique platform requiring content specific to its native environment, a lesson applicable to all social media platforms. For instance, content that works well on Instagram may not work as well on LinkedIn, Facebook, or TikTok.

A crucial part of Duolingo's story is that their TikTok campaign didn't merely generate views and likes. It significantly impacted their business, catapulting them to the number one education app in the Apple store. Like many other apps, Duolingo has a paid version, so this elevated status positively impacted their revenue.

The Importance of Social Media for Marketing

Duolingo's success story illustrates precisely why every company should be on social media in one form or another. However, which social media platforms your business utilizes will ultimately depend on your industry and where your audience spends their time. At the end of this chapter, we'll help you understand the audience types for each platform.

Once you decide which platforms are worth your time, determine how best to use them. The content your company will share should be greatly predetermined by your creative brief and content calendar. However, it is important to understand how often you can commit to posting. Will you advertise on the platform? If so, how will this differ from your organic posting strategy?

Social media marketing offers many benefits. It can generate awareness for your product (a top-of-the-funnel tactic), support the customer journey, provide opportunities to showcase your brand's culture, facilitate conversations with your customers and prospects, and support other content strategies, such as blog posts and videos.

Social media networks are treasure troves of data, tracking users' activities within their platforms and across the web, making it easier to target your audience effectively. Everyone, from CEOs to seven-year-olds, is on social media. You just need the right content and accurate targeting to reach your ideal audience.

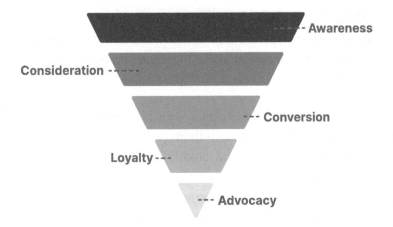

This figure depicts several steps in the customer journey. Social media builds top of funnel Awareness for your product and service. That phase then supports and nurtures the customer through the Consideration phase which ultimately leads to the decision to purchase, or the Conversion phase. From there, you can improve retention through content that creates Loyalty. Loyal customers then become advocates for your brand and referral resources in the Advocacy phase.

Social media isn't only for building top-of-funnel awareness; it's also an excellent tool for supporting the entire customer journey. As your customers progress through making a purchase, your social media presence can provide ongoing support.

Social media also offers unique opportunities for brands. You can reveal your brand identity, showcasing your company culture to attract talented employees and build customer relationships. Customers and clients are likelier to buy from brands they like and identify with.

Finally, social media supports other content strategies. It's an ideal platform for amplifying your search engine–optimized blogs and video content. In the ever-evolving digital marketing landscape, integrating social media into your overall strategy is no longer optional; it's essential.

Note: When deciding which platforms your business should utilize, I suggest revisiting your creative brief to consider your target audience and the platforms they frequent. Although every social media platform has a diverse demographic, some attract different demographics more than others—so be sure to also factor in the content calendar. Based on your target audience and the content calendar, you can determine which platforms will benefit your marketing efforts the most.

The Difference Between Organic vs. Paid Content

Now that you understand the importance of social media in your marketing, let's dive into the difference between organic and paid strategies. Both have their advantages and disadvantages, but it's crucial to understand their unique attributes and how they can serve your business objectives.

Organic Posts

Organic posts have the advantage of being cost-free. They allow brands to share content without requiring an advertising budget. However, more established platforms like Facebook and Instagram have algorithms that make it difficult for organic posts from brands to gain visibility unless they have a large following and garner a significant amount of engagement. So, the main drawback of organic postings is that their reach is often limited.

Most times, to increase visibility on these platforms, you must pay to play. These social media companies generate revenue by encouraging businesses to advertise with them, suppressing organic posts, to an extent, and promoting paid ones.

Paid Posts

This brings us to paid posts, a method that offers numerous benefits. First and foremost, paid postings overcome the visibility hurdle organic posts face. Even though there's a cost involved, it's important to note that these platforms make advertising relatively affordable compared to other media types. A budget of several hundred dollars can potentially put your brand in front of thousands of prospective customers. At the same time, a budget of five figures or more can garner millions of impressions for your targeted audience.

The main distinction between organic and paid posts is visibility. Organic posts are often suppressed, making it challenging for users to see them. In contrast, paid posts are prioritized because they generate revenue for the platform.

Paid or promoted posts can drastically increase your content's visibility, enhancing engagement in likes, comments, and website click-throughs. They also unlock various advanced features that can fine-tune your marketing efforts.

These advertising features utilize big data in shaping the effectiveness of social media advertising targeting. With the massive volume of user-generated content, interactions, and behaviors across platforms like Facebook, Instagram, and LinkedIn, advertisers can leverage big data to optimize their targeting strategies in the following ways:

- **Audience segmentation.** Big data enables advertisers to segment their target audience more accurately. Advertisers can create highly specific audience segments by analyzing user demographics, interests, behaviors, and preferences. This segmentation helps ensure that the right content is delivered to the right people, maximizing the chances of engagement and conversion

- **Behavioral targeting.** Big data allows advertisers to track user behaviors on social media platforms. This includes understanding what content users engage with, what they search for, and how they interact with posts and ads. Advertisers can use this data to create behavioral profiles, enabling them to tailor their messaging to align with user interests and behaviors

- **Personalization.** Social media platforms collect vast amounts of data about user preferences and interactions. With big data analysis, advertisers can personalize ads to an individual level. Ad content, images, and calls to action can be customized based on a user's past interactions and preferences, leading to higher engagement rates and conversions.

- **Lookalike audiences.** Big data facilitates the creation of lookalike audiences. Advertisers can identify the characteristics and behaviors of their most valuable customers and use this information to find similar audiences within the platform's user base. This approach helps expand the potential reach of a campaign while maintaining relevancy.

- **Real-time optimization.** Social media platforms generate real-time data on user interactions and ad performance. Big data tools can process this information rapidly, allowing advertisers to adjust their targeting and campaign strategies on the fly. Advertisers can quickly pivot to a different approach if a segment is not responding as expected.

- **Predictive analytics.** Big data enables predictive analytics by analyzing historical data and patterns. Advertisers can anticipate user behavior and tailor their campaigns accordingly. For instance, predictive analytics can help identify the best times to post content or the type likely to resonate most with a particular audience segment.

- **Ad placement optimization.** Big data analysis can reveal which platforms, channels, and placements are most effective for different audience segments. Advertisers can allocate their budgets more efficiently by focusing on the channels that yield the highest return on investment.

- **Sentiment analysis.** Big data allows advertisers to monitor social media conversations and sentiment about their brand, products, or industry. This sentiment analysis can guide advertisers in crafting campaigns that address specific concerns or capitalize on positive trends.

Paid social media marketing utilizes big data and empowers advertisers to fine-tune their targeting strategies in previously unimaginable ways. By leveraging the wealth of information available on user behavior, preferences, and interactions, advertisers can create highly personalized and effective campaigns that resonate with their target audience, leading to better engagement, conversion rates, and overall campaign success.

TikTok Is an Outlier

There is, however, one notable exception to this rule: TikTok.

TikTok offers more visibility for organic content, but that will likely change over time as the platform matures and shifts toward monetization. Therefore, while the general trend leans toward the need for paid postings for visibility, TikTok remains a space where organic reach can still provide significant results.

As you shape your social media strategy, be mindful of each platform's organic and paid dynamics. When used correctly, these tools can help you reach your audience more effectively and create a stronger brand presence on social media.

Selecting the Right Social Media Platforms

Social media is a fundamental part of daily life. With millions of active users across various platforms, it gives businesses countless opportunities to connect with their audiences. But which social media platforms should marketers focus on? We recommend four of the most popular:

Facebook: The Digital Marketing Staple

Many people view Facebook as a necessary evil in digital marketing. Facebook has been around forever, and some people may think it's fading off, mainly appealing to older generations.

However, it remains a vital tool in digital marketing. It's worth having a Facebook page for your business; keeping the page updated is extremely important. Customers often look to Facebook for business updates: When are you open? Where are you located? Do you have multiple locations? They also use your page for customer service issues, to leave reviews, and to interact with other customers.

A Facebook page also opens a gateway to advanced advertising opportunities on Facebook and Instagram. Advertising on Facebook can drive impressive results for increased impressions, engagement, and link clicks, often at a relatively low cost. Despite the misconceptions, Facebook continues to dominate the digital advertising world. When writing this book, Facebook still boasts the largest user base among all social media platforms, nationally and globally.

Instagram: The Visual Powerhouse

Instagram has evolved significantly since its inception, yet it has remained relevant to marketers throughout all its updates. At its core, Instagram is designed to share visually appealing content through still images, graphics, or videos.

The use of Instagram varies for B2B and B2C companies. Instagram is necessary for B2C or D2C brands, providing an excellent platform for building an online community or generating engagement. Many customers of restaurants, hospitality, retail, and other B2C verticals rely on Instagram for a quick peek at what they can expect from a business.

B2B companies can utilize Instagram to showcase their culture (crucial for recruiting), philanthropy, client work (especially useful for creative firms like architects, designers, and contractors), and thought leadership content. Thus, Instagram's emphasis on aesthetics offers businesses a platform to share their story and values in an engaging, attractive way.

LinkedIn: The Professional Social Network

LinkedIn is unique as it caters to a specific user—business professionals. Yet, it seems to be quite underrated in digital marketing. B2C brands should use LinkedIn to showcase partnership opportunities, employment openings, innovative ideas, and philanthropic endeavors. (The same goes for B2B companies as well.) Your business's LinkedIn page should post a mix of content, from company updates and culture pieces to industry insights and service promotions.

LinkedIn also offers advanced advertising capabilities, targeting specific job titles, company industries, and company names. If used correctly, LinkedIn can generate a high volume of clicks at a low cost, making the most out of any advertising budget. This platform is more than a networking tool, however: it's a powerful marketing instrument marketers should not overlook.

TikTok: The New Frontier

TikTok, one of the newest players on the social media scene, is one platform many businesses and marketers are reluctant to try out. The reason? It challenges our habit of repurposing content across social media platforms. What works on other platforms simply does not work as is on TikTok. It demands short-form video content, so you must change how you deliver and repurpose content accordingly.

Although there are many different video formats, TikTok's is almost templated. Following trends, such as closed captioning and popular sounds, is necessary to get your video noticed and appear on users' feeds.

TikTok also allows targeting users based on their interaction with organic content, ensuring that your ads reach highly engaged users. It's a platform where businesses can entertain, inform, inspire, and showcase their culture, creating impactful brand recognition. TikTok's user base is also incredibly large and diverse, so it's still worth exploring even if you think TikTok doesn't work for your business or industry.

The Selection Process: Why These Platforms?

With the numerous social media platforms available, why focus on Facebook, Instagram, LinkedIn, and TikTok specifically? It comes down to a balance of audience size, engagement opportunities, and unique characteristics that make these platforms ideal for business marketing.

Facebook: Universal Reach

Facebook's sheer user base is massive, with billions of active users monthly, making it a platform with universal reach.

Instagram: Visual Storytelling

Instagram's emphasis on visually appealing content has made it a preferred platform for businesses that want to tell their story in a more aesthetic and engaging manner. It's a perfect platform for brands to showcase products in action.

LinkedIn: Professional Engagement

LinkedIn's catering to professionals and business audiences makes it an ideal platform for B2B marketing. Businesses can professionally connect with industry peers, potential hires, and even prospective customers.

TikTok: Trend-Driven Engagement

TikTok has introduced a new way of engaging audiences through short, creative, and often entertaining videos. This platform's trend-driven nature makes it a fertile ground for businesses willing to step outside traditional marketing boundaries.

Why Not Include YouTube and X?

YouTube

While YouTube undoubtedly has a massive user base and high engagement, its position as a social media platform is not as clear cut as one might think. In many ways, YouTube functions more as a search engine (being the second-largest search engine after Google, its parent company). The emphasis on YouTube is content discovery through search, not necessarily social interactions.

X

X (formerly Twitter) is an ideal platform for real-time updates and direct communication with followers without media interruption. Many government departments and nonprofits use X specifically to share important updates. It can also be an excellent tool for businesses to publish updates, such as closures or outages, or to provide another way for customers to contact a service representative. However, unlike the other social networks we recommend, it's not typically the best platform for targeted advertising.

Social Media Marketing Principles and Best Practices

Ensuring your social media strategy is effective involves adhering to certain best practices:

Refer to Your Creative Brief

Always keep your target audience in mind when crafting your messages. It ensures that your content resonates with them, leading to higher engagement.

Plan Ahead

Prepare your content in advance to maintain a consistent posting schedule. While some posts may be spontaneous in response to real-time events, having a content calendar assures a consistent flow. You can plan weeks or months ahead, an especially salient factor for larger brands with stringent compliance requirements.

Experiment and Test

Leverage the A/B testing capabilities of these platforms to optimize your content. Test different types of content (like images vs. videos, long- vs. short-form text) and varied audience segments to find what yields the best results.

Measure and Monitor

Regularly track the performance of your content. This helps you understand what's working and what's not, providing valuable insights to refine your strategy further.

Conclusion

As the landscape of digital marketing evolves, so too should your strategies. Harnessing the power of these social media platforms is no longer a "nice-to-have" but a critical component of successful marketing. Each platform offers unique advantages that, when effectively utilized, can amplify your brand's message, engage your target audience, and drive business growth.

Whether it's through Facebook's universal reach, Instagram's visual storytelling, LinkedIn's professional engagement, or TikTok's trend-driven content, it's clear that social media has an enormous role to play in shaping a successful digital marketing strategy.

Social Media Evaluation Questions

Now that we've discussed how to run a successful social campaign, evaluate your current social media campaigns by considering the following:

- Are you using the right social media platforms to reach your target audience?

- Are your social media profiles complete and consistent with your brand image?

- Are you posting consistently and engaging with your audience?

- Do your social media posts align with your overall marketing strategy and brand guidelines?

- Are you monitoring and analyzing the performance of your social media campaigns? How many visitors do your social profiles and campaigns receive? What about engagement? Do your posts have likes, comments, and shares?

U8

Chapter 8
Harness the Marketing Power of Email

This chapter emphasizes the importance of using a tried-and-true digital marketing technique, email, as one component in an integrated campaign development plan.

When we talk to clients about email marketing, often their eyes glaze over like, "Really, are we talking about email as a digital marketing tactic? Haven't people been doing this since the beginning of the internet?" The answer is yes; email is probably one of the earliest digital tactics utilized by nearly every size and type of business.

What they don't understand is that email provides the highest ROI of any tactics discussed in this book. Sending out emails monthly or even daily is relatively inexpensive compared to other marketing tactics. It's also evergreen. Emails can live in an inbox for a long time, depending on the user. Messages don't often get deleted, even the ones the recipient doesn't read.

Email is also much more dynamic now than in the past. Over time, it has progressed to include graphics, animations, polls—you name it. Email is also more personalized than it used to be, from consumer names and birthdays in subject lines to curated items within the email that they may be interested in purchasing. This all works to continuously grab the consumer's attention, even as new digital advertising mediums arise.

Email lists often comprise individuals who have already purchased from your company or are considering doing so. This presents a highly valuable segment: current or prospective customers already familiar with your brand and offerings.

Whenever I do a speaking engagement, I ask the audience, "How many of you check your email daily?" The answer is everyone.

Your inbox is where you can reliably find your target audience almost every day of the year. For brands, this makes email marketing indispensable. With the proper planning, use of your creative calendar, and other tactics like the long-form content you create, you can put together an email quickly and send it out easily.

Such was the case with one of our clients, a D2C consumable products company.

The company had a loyal customer base and a product that required repurchasing weekly or monthly, depending on the frequency of use. The client and product had been around for a while and were among the top five vendors in a very competitive industry. However, even though they were selling nationally through some of the largest retailers in the United States, they lacked the same traction as their competitors digitally.

Their messaging was convoluted, and their website had an outdated user interface. We fixed those problems, but looking closer, we noticed they lacked an effective email marketing strategy, so we took several steps to up their game.

We created different product offerings and understood the discounts the client could provide. We also subscribed to their competitors' emails to better grasp how they promoted their products. We then benchmarked their discounts and email frequency and created a matrix to show the client how the competition was utilizing email and promotions.

Next, we focused on list segmentation. The client had accumulated over seventy-five thousand email addresses as part of their digital marketing strategy. Despite being a large amount of data, none of it was segmented. So, we segmented the list into relevant target audience groups.

The power of segmentation lies in its ability to classify customers into similar groups based on their buying behaviors, demographics, product or service use, and other factors. This process enables you to create campaigns tailored to specific audiences within your database.

We utilized the client's point-of-sale and e-commerce software data to create three distinct customer groups:

1. **Keepers**
   These are loyal customers who purchase the product regularly, once a week or more. Retaining these customers, the highest revenue source, was paramount. This group loved the product; there was little chance they were going anywhere else, so we designed loyalty programs (sent to them via email) that included customer loyalty rebates and bulk discounts to keep them engaged and satisfied.

2. Recaptures

This group consisted of formerly loyal customers who had purchased the product at least four times but hadn't purchased it in over three months. We realized these customers likely chose a competitor's lower-cost product instead of completely stopping usage. Recapturing them became a primary focus because they were still in the market for products like ours, leading us to develop the "We Want You Back" campaign that included discounts and content designed to win them back.

3. One-time Buyers

These customers had made an initial purchase or only bought once and never returned. We developed special promotions and content specifically targeted at these individuals to make them repeat buyers.

The insights we gained from the list segmentation enabled us to create campaigns to extend the loyalty of the client's regular customers, win back old customers, and convert more first-time buyers into regulars. The outcome was a 42 percent increase in year-over-year sales from email marketing alone.

Choosing the Right Email Marketing Platform

Email is an integral part of a broader digital marketing strategy. Choosing the right email-sending platform can significantly impact your email marketing efforts' effectiveness. However, not all platforms are created equal. There are dozens to choose from.

The choice of a platform depends on your internal systems, budget, and industry. Using platforms like MailChimp or Constant Contact is a no-brainer for most businesses. However, more advanced platforms like HubSpot and Marketo integrate marketing automation and customer relationship management. There are even industry-specific platforms, like Klaviyo, for e-commerce.

We recommend researching various platforms to see which makes the most sense for your business. One thing is for sure: You can't send these emails out of your Outlook or Gmail efficiently without crashing your servers. They are not designed or intended for bulk email distribution.

Criteria for Selecting an Email Marketing Platform

The choice of the platform depends on a variety of factors, including the following:

List Size

Depending on the size of your email list, you might need a platform that can handle a large volume of emails without a glitch.

Frequency

How often you send emails can affect the platform you choose. If you send messages daily, you need a platform that can handle high frequency.

Function

The functionality you need—a simple email-sending service or a more advanced automation platform—can influence your choice.

Cost

Your budget also plays a crucial role in determining which platform to select. While some are very inexpensive, others can cost thousands of dollars per month or more.

Email Marketing Principles and Best Practices

There are certain principles and best practices you should consider to ensure your email marketing efforts are effective.

Determine the Right Frequency and Content

How often should you appear in your audience's inbox, and what should you share? Your content and frequency dictate the success of your email marketing strategy.

Thought leadership content, like blogs and videos, works well for B2B companies. For B2C and D2C companies, promotions and calls to action are more effective. Remember, your content should be valuable and relevant to your audience. Monitor it carefully to avoid overwhelming subscribers.

You have already outlined a creative strategy, which you can utilize where content is concerned. Frequency should relate to how much content you have available. Too much frequency can increase unsubscribe rates. Too little, and customers forget about you.

You can also base frequency on customer purchasing behaviors. For example, if yours is a product or service I always use, then a daily and weekly email is suggested. However, a daily email will be overkill if I only use your products or services annually. The content may not be relevant.

Pro tip: Measure if a campaign is hitting that right frequency-to-content ratio by looking at three metrics: unsubscribe, open, and click-through rates. These metrics will reveal whether you're spamming or being too infrequent.

Keep Messages Short and Simple

We find that the correct email length is essential. A short, skimmable email keeps readers engaged and interested. The click-through rate is better than with longer emails, which can become too convoluted and harder to understand where the call to action is concerned.

Include Visuals

Images, infographics, and other visual content can make your emails more attractive and engaging and break up the monotony of a text-only message.

Craft Compelling Subject Lines

Your subject line is the first thing recipients see and is what will get your reader to open the emails. Subject lines should be concise, enticing, and accurately represent the content contained in the message. A good subject line should be easy to figure out if you have great content to pair with it. Length is particularly important: you don't want the subject line to be so long that it's cut off or people won't know what you're trying to say.

Segment Your Audience

We discussed the power of segmentation in the example at the beginning of the chapter, but let's expand on why you should segment.

Proper list segmentation will enable you to create email campaigns to increase revenue and conversions. Instead of sending to everyone, focus on sending content to the right target audience. Relevance is key and will result in higher open and click-through rates. No one wants to get irrelevant emails. That's called spam.

Ways to segment include the following:

- **Purchase behaviors.** That could be frequent buyers versus seasonal buyers versus one-time-only buyers.

- **Demographics.** Location, age, and gender are examples of demographics to consider.

- **Brand-centric.** Create segments you feel are essential for your brand that will increase open and click-through rates and decrease unsubscribe rates.

Create Triggered and Automated Campaigns

A triggered campaign is when an email is automatically sent based on someone taking action, such as filling out a quote form before making their first purchase. Another example is an email sent on a customer's birthday to wish them a happy birthday, including a special offer.

Email series are an example of an automated campaign. You might put someone into an email series based on location, purchasing behavior, or customer journey. Depending on where they are in the sales funnel, you can send messages that educate, create a desire for your products or services, and ask for a sale.

Clean the List Regularly

It's important to send emails only to people who are engaged. It can impact the health of your open, bounce, and click-through rates if you keep many inactive users who haven't touched an email in months. You can easily set up a campaign to reengage inactive users but remove them from your list if they remain dormant or give them the option to re-opt in, ensuring they want to continue receiving your content.

While emails are inexpensive, they aren't free. Most email-sending platforms charge you based on the number of subscribers on your list and the volume of emails you send, so it makes economic sense to keep it clean.

Conclusion

When done right, email marketing can be a powerful digital marketing channel. It provides a cost-effective and straightforward way to reach your audience, nurture relationships, and drive conversions. By understanding your audience, choosing the right platform, and adhering to best practices, you can leverage email marketing to its fullest potential.

Email Marketing Evaluation Questions

Now that we've discussed how to run a successful email marketing campaign, evaluate your current efforts by considering the following questions:

- How often do you send emails to customers and prospects?
- Are you segmenting your email lists based on customer preferences and behavior?
- Does the content of your email campaigns provide value to your subscribers?
- Are you testing and optimizing your email subject lines and content?
- Are you tracking and analyzing critical metrics like open rates, click-through rates, unsubscribes, and conversions?

- Are you complying with relevant email marketing regulations, such as GDPR or CAN-SPAM?

- Do you regularly "clean up" your contact list to ensure optimal metrics like open rate and clicks?

U9

Chapter 9
Amplify Your Strategy with CTV and OTT Media Buying

This chapter familiarizes the reader with CTV and OTT media buying, defines key terms, discusses pros and cons, and outlines best practices to maximize these emerging marketing opportunities.

In an era where technology rapidly alters the consumer landscape, businesses must constantly evolve their marketing mix to stay relevant. Enter media buying for CTV (Connected TV) and OTT (over-the-top), a newer facet of digital marketing that grants access to highly targeted audience segments and allows for more refined success metrics.

CTV refers to television sets connected to the internet that enable viewers to access streaming content, apps, and online services through platforms like smart TVs, streaming devices (such as Roku, Amazon Fire TV, and Apple TV), and gaming consoles. CTV allows users to watch on-demand videos, live TV, and streaming services, providing a more personalized and flexible viewing experience that bridges the gap between traditional television and digital content.

OTT refers to the delivery of video content and other media services directly to viewers over the internet, bypassing traditional cable, satellite, or broadcast television platforms. OTT services provide a wide range of on-demand content, including movies, TV shows, documentaries, and original programming, accessible through devices such as smart TVs, smartphones, tablets, computers, and streaming devices. Examples of popular OTT services include Netflix, Hulu, Amazon Prime Video, and Disney+. OTT has disrupted the traditional television landscape, offering viewers greater flexibility and control over what they watch and when they watch it.

The main difference lies in the consumption medium: CTV is device specific, focusing on internet-connected televisions, while OTT is channel or show specific, serving content via apps that the user accesses across various devices. The following table showcases the differences between OTT and CTV:

Feature	OTT	CTV
Definition	Video content delivered over the internet	A television or TV device connected to the internet to deliver OTT content
Examples	Netflix, Hulu, Amazon Prime Video, Disney+	Smart TV's, TVs connected to streaming devices, or gaming consoles
Target Audience	Cord cutters, people who want to watch more on demand	People who want to watch on demand content on television or large display
Advertising	Targeted content across a user's favorite app, channel, or show	Targeted content based on a user's demographic, location, or brand affinity

The decision between CTV or OTT isn't either-or. Rather, it's about understanding how these elements interact within your broader marketing strategy. Because CTV targets the devices viewers use, while OTT targets the specific apps and channels on those devices, it's common for a comprehensive media buying strategy to leverage both.

US Connected TV (CTV) Ad Spending, 2021-2027

billions, % change, and % of digital ad spending

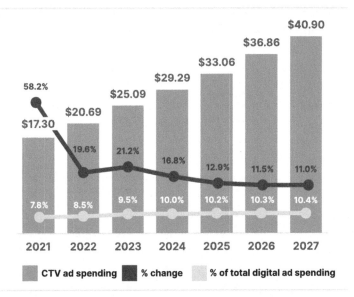

Note: digital advertising that appears on CTV devices; includes display ads that appear on home screens and in-streamvideo ads that appear on CTVs from platforms like Hulu, Roku, and Youtube; excludes network-sold inventory from traditional linear TV and addressable TV advertising.
Source: eMarketing, March 2023

Popular CTV and OTT Success Stories

Typical goals of CTV and OTT are driving brand awareness and increasing sales. Volvo did just that in the promotion of its S90 vehicle.

In 2021, Volvo produced an interactive video ad highlighting the car's exterior and interior and delivered it across Roku and Samsung devices. The ad featured personalized location-based messages, encouraging, for example, New Jersey viewers to visit a dealership in New Jersey. The ad also guided viewers to a landing page where they could subscribe to SMS messages for more information. The campaign resulted in half a million unique engagements, twelve hundred requests for more information through text, and reached almost one hundred thousand households. Most impressively, Volvo experienced a 35 percent sales lift attributable to a single ad across two publishers.

In another example, the Atlanta Hawks basketball team used a CTV campaign to boost ticket sales. Their strategy involved creating two narrative commercials. Within a few days of watching one of the commercials, viewers would see an ad urging them to buy tickets for an upcoming game. Using first- and second-party data to target sports lovers and live event–goers in Georgia, the Hawks managed to drive a 25 percent ticket site visit rate from viewers who saw the commercials.

These success stories underscore the potential of media buying as a value-add to any marketing mix.

The Strategic Role of Media Buying in Marketing

Everything we discuss in this book is about being in front of the targeted audience where they are, whether in Google when they are searching, in their inbox when they open an email, or on social media when they scroll through their feed. Media buying gives us yet another opportunity to reach that targeted audience with higher-end, curated creative content.

Media buying's effectiveness lies in the principle of frequency, the number of times you reach a target audience. People get a ton of content thrown at them every day. For that reason, it's very easy to forget about a brand they have only seen a few times. Understanding where your audience is (not where you *think* they are) and ensuring you place creative marketing collateral strategically (where they will want to see it) makes your brand more memorable.

With the advent of CTV and OTT, media buying extends beyond traditional advertising. Unlike typical TV commercials, which can play to an empty room or disinterested viewer, CTV and OTT ads appear on highly engaged programs. Targeting viewers with a video you think they would be interested in when they're choosing to sit down and pay attention increases the likelihood that they will watch the ad all the way through, creating a more intimate and memorable interaction.

CTV/OTT: The New Digital Marketing Frontier

CTV and OTT represent a significant change from traditional media buying, allowing advertisers to be more targeted with their campaigns.

In an earlier chapter, I mentioned that Kraus Marketing has had the privilege of partnering with some of the largest companies in the world. We have also worked with emerging contenders aiming for the top spots in their respective categories. One such company, a professional services firm currently ranked among the top twenty in their industry nationally, approached us with a desire to break into the top ten and, eventually, the top five brands for their category.

The company had experienced exponential growth over the past fifteen years but faced a significant challenge: brand recognition. Despite their achievements, the broader market was largely unaware of their brand. The firm's CMO described their situation this way: "Our CEO likes to call us the best-kept secret, but I despise that label. How can we shed this 'secret' status?"

Enter CTV and OTT advertising.

When the CMO expressed her desire for enhanced brand awareness and lead generation, we introduced her to the potential offered by CTV and OTT. We told her that CTV and OTT allow for precise targeting, unlike traditional "shotgun advertising," which broadly targets audiences to reach the right demographic. This approach was especially crucial for our client, who, despite having a substantial seven-figure budget, was competing against industry giants with much deeper pockets.

Our proposal was simple yet strategic: leverage CTV and OTT advertising to reach their exact target audience on their main televisions and handheld devices. This approach would ensure optimal use of their budget by focusing solely on potential clients and stakeholders.

The campaign we designed spanned thirty days and featured:

- Thirty- and fifteen-second videos placed on streaming channels and mobile devices, tailored to the target audience's preferences and behaviors.

- Display ad remarketing, ensuring that users who encountered a CTV or OTT ad would subsequently see native display ads on news and business websites.

The results were nothing short of remarkable. The key performance indicators (KPIs) just thirty days from campaign start were:

- A staggering 900,000 total impressions, indicating the number of times the creatives were displayed on users' devices.

- 2,900 site visits, facilitated by QR codes on CTV or direct click-throughs on OTT and display remarketing ads.

- One hundred contact form submissions from users who engaged with the ads.

- A 95 percent surge in new users on the campaign landing page; a significant jump from their previous efforts, which were limited to social media advertising.

The client was happy with these numbers and amazed at how quickly it affected their brand recognition and top-line revenue. As the CTV and OTT media buy continued, it became a game changer for this client, transforming the company from an industry "secret" to a recognized and respected brand.

The Advantage of CTV and OTT over Traditional Broadcast Commercials

The real value of CTV and OTT lies in their targeted approaches to audience engagement and the data-driven insights they provide.

With traditional media buying, you purchase inventory based on where you think your target audience might be. For instance, a B2B company may say that their customers watch CNBC, so they buy inventory on CNBC. Or they think customers watch HGTV, so they buy a spot on HGTV. That results in many wasted impressions as ads may be displayed to irrelevant viewers, such as a child watching an ad targeting adults or even ads running on screens when no one is watching. CTV and OTT advertising, on the other hand, utilizes first- and second-party data to serve ads to specific audiences based on their behaviors and interests, much like ad buying on social media.

Beyond precise targeting, CTV and OTT advertising provide actionable data and measurable results.

We recently met with a client we were talking to about traditional and paid advertising. When we asked the client how they would measure the success of broadcast television, they had no clue. With CTV and OTT, we have actual data and engagement metrics to measure a campaign's success.

Metrics such as view-through rate, or VTR (how much of your ad was viewed to completion), can provide valuable insight into campaign performance. CTV ads boast a VTR rate upward of 85% compared to traditional broadcast TV's estimated viewability rate of 40–50%. CTV and OTT allow for a more cost-effective, precise, and data-driven approach to reaching potential customers.

You can also measure based on interactivity using QR codes, landing pages, phone numbers, and text messages. On the other hand, you throw out an ad on traditional broadcast television and see if it sticks.

While it is possible to include QR codes in broadcast ads, CTV and OTT enable better attribution. For example, you can add pixels to landing pages and track whether users have arrived from specific commercials or creative out-puts. CTV ads' viewability and interaction rates are notably higher, making them a better investment than broadcast in most cases.

Pros and Cons of CTV and OTT

Before fully appreciating CTV and OTT advertising's poten-tial, you must also understand the possible setbacks. The cons fall under how you go about it, and that starts with understanding your audience. If you don't understand your audience for targeting purposes, there's a good chance you won't see a reasonable ROI. Incorrect targeting can also lead to oversaturation, especially if the publisher already has high traffic volume.

The recency of the technology is another potential draw-back. While streaming platforms' user bases (also known as cord-cutters) are steadily growing, they are less extensive than traditional broadcast TV.

Despite these challenges, CTV and OTT offer significant advantages, including using AI and big data to hyper-target audience segments and measure interactions. In contrast to traditional television, you can track engagement and tweak your campaigns in real time. This gives you the unique ability to measure the success of a campaign beyond simple viewership figures.

Decoding CTV and OTT Terminology

Like many forms of digital marketing and advertising, media buying has a unique vocabulary, especially concerning CTV and OTT. Here are some of the more common terms:

- **Programmatic:** This term refers to the automatic bidding system for ad placements. It helps ensure your ads hit the right spots and that your budget can compete in different spaces, such as Hulu or Netflix.

- **Big data:** Big data involves complex data sets that traditional data processing application software cannot handle. In advertising you can use big data to gain insights into consumer behavior and trends.

- **Behavioral interest targeting:** This term refers to serving ads to people based on their past behavior. For example, if a user often watches car shows, they might see more ads for car companies and accessories.

- **Conquesting:** This is a competitive tactic where you target your ads to users who have shown interest in your competitors' products or services. For example, if someone is receiving email communication from a competitor, you can target them with your CTV or OTT ads. Or, if a competitor shows an audience member a commercial, you can ensure the person sees one of your ads as well.

Finally, to make the most out of CTV and OTT advertising, it's essential to be selective with your publishers. Different platforms have unique viewer demographics, and the right choice can substantially affect your campaign's effectiveness. Whether you're running ads around a large sporting event or just bidding on general placements, a granular, data-driven approach will lead to more successful outcomes.

CTV and OTT Principles and Best Practices

Understand the Target Audience and Customer Journey

The first fundamental principle of media buying is thoroughly understanding your target audience and their customer journey. Media buying is a targeted investment, not a random expense. Knowing precisely when and where to reach your audience will enhance their retention of the ad and increase the likelihood of a return on investment.

You should align your media buying strategy with the customer journey to boost the effectiveness of your campaign. If budgets allow, setting up campaigns that target users at various stages of this journey, such as brand awareness, interest, conversion, and retargeting, is recommended. Further, test the most effective way to get new users, such as broad audience targeting, interest targeting, or lookalike audiences.

Adopt an Omnichannel Approach and Budget Management

Another media buying best practice involves taking an omnichannel approach and being mindful of your budget. Creating a media plan with multiple touchpoints prevents reliance on a single placement or buy. Diverse channels can reach the same user at different stages of their customer journey, making consistent messaging across all channels a critical factor.

It's essential to consider varying costs depending on placement, targeting, and timeline. While it can be beneficial to cast a wide net at the start of a campaign (across channels and audiences), strategic budget allocation, placements, and targeting can significantly influence your campaign's success. After all, great creative won't mean anything if a well-thought-out campaign setup does not back it.

Measure and Report

Lastly, effective reporting and measurement mechanisms are essential to successful media buying. Before launching a campaign, establish a clear list of KPIs that align with your brand's goals and ensure they can be effectively measured. That could involve tools like pixel event tracking within an ad platform or Google Analytics. It's best to have multiple ways to track and cross-reference KPIs, especially with the continued changes to online privacy regulations.

Treat initial media buys as an A/B test, adjusting spending based on tangible metrics such as impressions, engagements, link clicks, or conversions. If a strategy or placement has been successful, measure the effectiveness of the media buy before phasing out others.

Besides measuring and optimizing the campaign's strategy and setup, report on ad creative. Testing at least two different creatives for each audience segment will provide an idea of what resonates most with users. Based on the results of an ad, you can determine what part of the creative is most effective or needs adjusting. Creative fatigue can occur if ads are not continuously optimized and refreshed throughout a campaign, driving up the total cost per campaign while decreasing results.

Conclusion

A strategic approach to CTV and OTT media buying involves a thorough understanding of your audience, a well-planned multi-channel strategy, and a robust system for measurement and reporting. This calculated, data-driven approach can help maximize your brand's presence across various media channels and ensure a profitable return on your investment.

As we move forward in this digital era, integrating CTV and OTT into your marketing strategy can offer a competitive edge, delivering tailored content to targeted audiences while providing valuable insights for continual strategy refinement. Embrace these newer tools to ensure your brand stands out in an increasingly crowded digital marketplace.

Part III
The Sharkbite Method™: Monitoring and Enhancing Your Efforts

How to analyze your business to successfully track and continue to grow the marketing initiatives discussed in part II.

10

Chapter 10
Digital Marketing Measurement and Campaign Optimization

This chapter underscores the need to measure relevant KPIs and ROI to determine campaign success. You will learn the importance of measuring, which KPIs to measure, and the best way to track metrics.

Over the years, my team at Kraus Marketing and I have found that without proper measurement you cannot understand which tactic is most impactful. It's not uncommon for clients to think they know what's going on with their website based on their gut feeling, but the analytics tell a different story.

In the early days, the "naysayers" thought what we did on their behalf wouldn't work. Whether it was a website that we said would get a couple of hundred thousand visits a month, an email campaign with a high percentage of opens and click-throughs, or a social media marketing campaign that would garner a substantial number of impressions, views, and engagements, we used analytics to prove the success of the strategy. They helped us measure what works and better understand where to spend our budgets properly.

The moral of this story is that you should measure everything you do.

The nice thing about the digital marketing we've discussed throughout this book is that it can all be measured. Google Analytics is one of the analytics platforms we use. The data it reveals tells a story about your marketing performance, how users are reached across different channels, and what ROI those efforts achieve.

Measuring Lifetime ROI

Return on investment is imperative for measuring your campaign's effectiveness and seeing where to make changes to maximize earning potential and efficiency—and whether it means increasing or decreasing budgets in certain areas.

Developing a concise strategy can help reduce the chances of dollars going to waste when beginning campaigns and ensure proper reporting and project surveillance stop poor business decisions before they happen. Making sure the right goals and metrics are in place to measure the success of a campaign can keep everyone on track and leave room for adjustment.

Something we like to discuss with our clients is measuring lifetime ROI (a client's lifespan) instead of ROI on any specific purchase. One of the easiest ways to show lifetime ROI is by using a simple formula, as shown in the following two figures: Customer Lifetime Value (CLV) divided by Customer Acquisition Cost (CAC).

Customer Lifetime Value

$$CLTV = \left[\begin{array}{c} \textbf{Customer Value} \\ \times \\ \textbf{Average Customer Lifespan} \end{array} \right]$$

CAC Formula
Customer Acquisition Cost

$$CAC = \frac{\textbf{(Cost of Sales + Cost of Marketing)}}{\textbf{New Customers Acquired}}$$

Finally, to calculate the ROI on Customer Lifetime Value, you utilize the following formula:

CLV ROI = CLV/CAC

CLV ROI equals the number of purchases per year times the average number of years you retain a customer divided by the customer acquisition cost, which is calculated by adding the cost of sales plus the cost of marketing and dividing that total by the number of customers acquired.

Once you start measuring CLV ROI, ad budgets are more easily justified. Where people fall short is that they measure the first sale for ROI. However, if your company provides more than just one-time services, the ROI will be much different when measured to reflect a CLV. Here are a few CLV ROI examples:

- **Car dealership:** On average, a car dealership makes only $2,000 on each vehicle it sells. And CAC is typically similar or more than that. However, if you use CLV, you would calculate that an average customer typically purchases two cars from you over six years and maintains that car several times yearly. The CLV of a six-year customer is much greater than that initial sale, providing an ROI worth the spend.

- **Law firm focusing on business law:** As an attorney, acquiring a new customer can be expensive, and sometimes the first assignment is a low-ticket item. For instance, if a new business customer came for help reviewing a business contract, that law firm might only make several hundred dollars. However, most law firms will tell you that business clients have several requests each year, equaling an average annual revenue of $10,000 or more—and those customers come back year after year. The customer lifetime value could easily reach six figures. Even with the higher marketing budgets required for this industry, one could understand why the spend is worth the investment.

It's essential when measuring ROI to look at the big picture. With some customers, we have even taken CLV a step further. There was a client with a successful real estate business, and he knew that they got one referral for every three customers they had. When calculating in the referral, their CLV went significantly higher and justified the extra spend that would support their agency's aggressive growth goals.

Knowing Which KPIs to Measure and How

When deciding which KPIs to measure, referring to your creative brief and campaign goals is best.

If one of your campaign goals is to increase revenue on your e-commerce store, a bottom-line KPI is e-commerce sales. From there you can measure which tactics contributed to the highest sales volume.

Another common metric for B2C and B2B firms is business leads. Typically, the conversions we measure for a lead are quote forms, phone calls, and emails. From there you must work backward to see which tactics created the most leads.

For the tactics that are not converting leads at a typical rate, you will want to look at two things:

1. **The creative you are serving.** Is it different than the creative from your other tactics? If so, realign the creative with better-performing tactics. This change should help improve performance.

2. **The audience you are targeting.** Review the audience targeting, as it is easy to make a mistake when setting up campaigns. The creative will not resonate appropriately if the target audience is incorrect.

Brand building is a common goal for larger companies. KPIs center around awareness and engagement. The form of impressions or visits typically measures awareness. At the same time, engagement is measured by time on site or interactions with your social channels.

When measuring KPIs, we compare present-day data to the historical data available. Two ways to do that are "current period" versus "previous period" and "year over year" (YoY). For many companies, year over year is the best point of comparison due to the cyclical nature of most sale patterns. On the other hand, you can use current period versus previous period to illustrate the effectiveness of a new campaign or media spend. Is your new creative performing better than your last campaign?

Below is a list of KPIs we commonly use to measure the effectiveness of our strategy.

Session Related KPIs

1. **New sessions vs. total sessions**

   Session tracking on web pages can be an extremely useful metric in measuring brand awareness and growth. "Sessions" pertaining to website tracking are classified within thirty-minute ranges in which a user is active on a website and doesn't include users who click a website and "bounce" off it quickly.

   • Tracking sessions can help identify user patterns, seasonal trends, and the effectiveness of landing pages in keeping users engaged and on the website.

2. **Engaged sessions**

   In contrast to a normal session, engaged sessions hold much higher value because to be qualified as "engaged," the session must last at least ten seconds, have a conversion event, or have at least two page views. Having a higher qualification for user interaction with the page gives a better representation of engagement and realistic measurement for those genuinely interacting with the site.

   • Having a website that is interactive, optimized for speed, and that provides engaging content will result in users spending more time on your web pages. Choosing a proper landing page is vital when backlinking your website on social media or in an email, as it can make or break user bounce rates.

3. **Engagement rate**

Engagement is an important metric in measuring interaction and involvement with your brand messaging and content, especially in the social media landscape, where consumers can be exposed to hundreds of advertisements and organic brand posts daily. Engagement shows the consumer's level of interest and can be a leading indicator of content issues when social media campaigns do not achieve the desired results.

- A good engagement rate for social platforms is between 1–5%. For websites, a reasonable engagement rate lies between 60–70%.

4. **Average engagement time**

Average engagement time is the length per website session your web page was in focus on a user's screen. This helps you understand how your website is actively being used and enables you to differentiate between someone just having a tab open/hidden or if someone is scrolling/clicking from page to page. A good average engagement time for a website visit is about sixty seconds.

- Much of the increasing engagement time comes from creating engaging content on your landing pages and ensuring a smooth user experience. Users are much more likely to stay engaged on a website with interesting content and easy navigation.

5. Click-through rate

Click-through rate (CTR) is vital in seeing the user flow through your produced content. This can directly correlate to the relevance of the content you market to viewers and how helpful they find the advertised message. It can also show whether your target audience is being reached depending on the level of CTR.

- Ensuring you provide relevant content to users increases their likelihood of clicking through more content on your platforms and accepting your credibility.

6. Geography

Knowing where sessions came from, geographically speaking, is very important to most companies. Companies that can only service regionally (e.g., industries like insurance, energy, or realty) would want to ensure that traffic comes from a user within their service area, while national firms will analyze traffic from stronghold areas compared to traffic in areas where they look to grow.

- Geography can drill down to continental, regional, state, and city levels. The detail you measure should relate to the target audience defined in your creative brief.

Source & Acquisition KPIs

7. Organic search ranking

Organic search ranking plays a vital role in the success of online businesses, given that the ranking is determined based on website content and relevance to the user search. Because Google tries to get users the answer to their questions as fast as possible, it filters out unqualified results and sends them further down the page in the search rankings, elevating the most qualified answers or results to the top. Optimizing site content, brand messaging, and user experience on your website can go a long way in making sure your business ranks in the appropriate place when users search for relevant products or services.

- Good practice for increasing your organic search ranking starts with building your website with relevant content and strategic keywords, optimizing site speed and user experience, and using quality backlinks to enhance credibility.

8. Source/medium

Source refers to where your website's traffic comes from (individual websites, Google, LinkedIn, Facebook, etc.), and Medium refers to how it got there (organic traffic, paid traffic, referral traffic, etc.). In Google Analytics, for example, this helps us define the channels that are a part of our marketing strategy and helps us build attribution models for our target audience.

- It's essential to always balance organic, paid, and social traffic. While paid content can deliver results instantly, organic can take time to build as a brand grows. Social traffic can vary, given the unpredictability of social trends. This can sometimes make for quick growth on social platforms if they are optimized correctly and relative content begins trending. It adds to the importance of keeping with trends across all marketing platforms and should reflect in the balance of a brand's sources and mediums.

9. **Customer journey attribution**

This term refers to measuring the most valuable touchpoints that lead to a website visit or conversion. Your marketing efforts should be omnichannel, meaning the use of several different strategies and/or channels to reach your target audience. Measure the channels performing the best; see where and when your audience prefers to be reached. If you cannot attribute success, it is difficult to manage success—as consumer behavior changes, what used to work may not always work.

- It's essential to set clear goals for customers as they continue through the journey, ensuring they are segmented, touchpoints are defined, and sufficient models are implemented to measure customer value as they progress.

Monetization KPIs

10. Conversion rate

Conversions are defined as when a user completes a goal upon visiting a website. These goals can be form submissions, button clicks, or purchases. The benefit of tracking conversions is that you can customize them to the specific goal or outcome you hope to achieve. This can better attribute value to certain occurrences on a business's website that might otherwise be overlooked.

For example, if a clothing company has a newly optimized product page and wants to track the results of the new user experience, it could value a conversion as clicks on the shopping category button to track its effectiveness and the customer interest it gains.

- Your conversion percentage can change based on desired outcomes and what the company classifies as a conversion. There is always room to optimize your strategy for gaining a conversion.

A/B Testing

A/B testing is a powerful technique used in marketing to optimize campaigns by comparing two variations, A and B, of a single element within the campaign to determine which one performs better in achieving a specific goal. Here are the steps to effectively utilize A/B testing to optimize your marketing campaign:

1. **Objective and hypothesis.**

   Define a clear objective for your marketing campaign, such as increasing click-through rates, conversions, or engagement. Based on this objective, formulate a hypothesis about what change could lead to better results. For instance, if you're sending an email newsletter, your hypothesis might be that changing the subject line to be more personalized will increase open rates.

2. **Element variation.**

   Identify a specific element within your campaign that you want to test. This could be a headline, image, call-to-action text, color scheme, layout, or any other element that could influence user behavior. Create two variations of this element: one represents the control (A), which remains unchanged, and the other is the variant (B), where you implement the specific change you hypothesized.

3. **Randomized testing.**

   Divide your target audience randomly into two groups: Group A and Group B. Group A will be exposed to the control version of the element, while Group B will see the variant version. It's crucial to ensure that the groups are similar in demographics, behavior, and other relevant characteristics to obtain reliable results.

   In social media, you may A/B test by serving up an ad utilizing two different graphics to the same target audience. For websites, many tools will randomize and measure A/B tests for landing pages.

4. Data collection and analysis.

Run your campaign with both element versions and collect relevant data based on your defined objective. That could include metrics like click-through rates, conversion rates, bounce rates, or time spent on a web page. After you reach a predetermined period or a significant sample size, analyze the data to determine which version performed better in achieving your objective. Statistical significance is crucial to ensure that any observed differences are not due to chance.

5. Implementation and iteration.

Once you've identified the version (A or B) that outperforms the other, implement it as the standard for your campaign. However, A/B testing doesn't stop here. As you optimize your marketing campaign, iterate and test other elements to refine your strategy further. Regularly revisit your hypotheses and try new variations to improve your campaign's performance over time.

A/B testing is a systematic approach that allows marketers to make data-driven decisions by comparing variations of campaign elements and measuring their impact on specific objectives.

Campaign Pivots

When reviewing your KPIs, you may find that a pivot is called for. As explained earlier in this chapter, identifying a KPI between tactics that are of statistical significance should lead you to first review the creative and target audiences set for the tactic.

If everything lines up, and it is obvious that one tactic performs substantially better than another, then a pivot may be in order.

For instance, you may find that social media users have a much higher conversion and engagement rate than pay-per-click users. For that reason, after significant attempts to optimize your pay-per-click campaign, you decide to pivot by lowering your pay-per-click budget and increasing your social media advertising budget.

In another example, upon review of your CTV and display-advertising KPIs, you notice that the CTR on display is lower than the CTR on CTV. The cost-per-click is also less for CTV, so you pivot by moving budget from display to CTV.

You can only know what campaign pivots to make when you measure correctly. Comparing KPIs from the different tactics within *The Sharkbite Method*™ will make it easy to recognize how to best optimize your campaign and spending. Remember that statistical significance is the key. That means ensuring there is enough data to support the change (time and disparity of data); once you've made the change, measure to ensure you achieve the hypothesis.

Use an Analytics Dashboard

The best way to monitor KPIs for a campaign is with an analytics dashboard, like those you find in Google Analytics.

Think of a dashboard as the homepage of your analytics software. It lets you quickly assess your website's and marketing campaign's performance.

You can create customized dashboards for each campaign depending on the analytics platform. Regardless, nearly every platform has some type of dashboard capability. We recommend including anywhere from seven to ten KPIs or even as many as fifteen if you want to dig deeper. Some platforms offer automated versions of dashboards that you can visit via your browser. There are also automated, templated reports you can create.

Reviewing your dashboard is like checking the oil in your car engine. It's something you do regularly. However, once a quarter, we recommend conducting a "100-point inspection" to get an in-depth view of how all your campaigns perform.

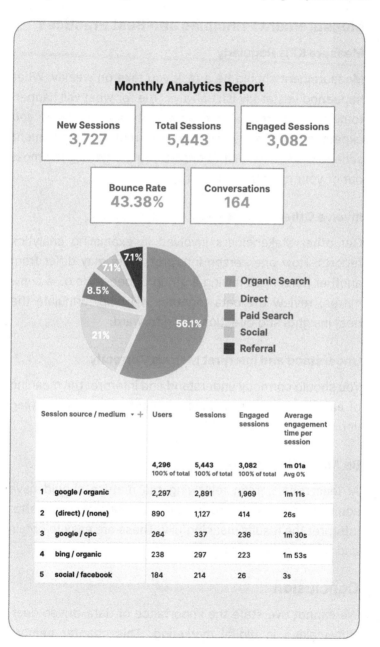

Monthly Analytics Report

New Sessions	Total Sessions	Engaged Sessions
3,727	5,443	3,082

Bounce Rate	Conversations
43.38%	164

- 56.1% Organic Search
- 21% Direct
- 8.5% Paid Search
- 7.1% Social
- 7.1% Referral

Session source / medium ▾ +	Users	Sessions	Engaged sessions	Average engagement time per session
	4,296 100% of total	5,443 100% of total	3,082 100% of total	1m 01a Avg 0%
1 google / organic	2,297	2,891	1,969	1m 11s
2 (direct) / (none)	890	1,127	414	26s
3 google / cpc	264	337	236	1m 30s
4 bing / organic	238	297	223	1m 53s
5 social / facebook	184	214	26	3s

Measurement Principles and Best Practices

Measure KPIs Regularly

Measurement should be a task you take on weekly. What happened yesterday isn't always true for what will happen tomorrow, so regular measurement is essential if you expect to reach your desired goals. Create a measurement schedule and stick to it to ensure you are getting the most out of your marketing budget.

Involve Other Stakeholders

Get other stakeholders involved in examining analytics reports. How one person interprets data may differ from another person, so having a group of people (e.g., a committee) review the data together will help formulate the best insights and direction going forward.

Understand and Interpret Metrics Correctly

You should correctly understand and interpret the meaning of each metric. You can't measure and analyze something you don't understand.

Be Analytics Certified

At least one person reviewing the metrics should have some type of marketing analytics certification to better interpret the results meaningfully. These are easy to obtain and most cost nothing.

Conclusion

We cannot overstate the importance of data-driven decision-making in digital marketing. This chapter demonstrates that measuring your marketing efforts' effectiveness validates your strategies and provides valuable insights to guide future campaigns. Whether it's determining your lifetime ROI or identifying the KPIs that will best reflect your campaign goals, data forms the bedrock upon which effective digital marketing is built.

Chapter 11
Understand Your Internal Data and Customer Insights

This chapter explores the crucial task of evaluating internal data and customer insights as part of a successful digital marketing campaign. By understanding the significance of this process, marketers can make informed decisions and create targeted strategies based on objective data and customer preferences. In addition, you will develop a baseline of where your business stands with your current digital efforts.

When we refer to internal data and customer insights, we are talking about the valuable information you possess within your organization to use in marketing strategies to make campaigns more effective. This data can come from various sources, such as accounting software, previous campaigns, and segmented email marketing lists. It encompasses all the information you have at your disposal to effectively target your audience—both existing and prospective customers.

For example, within your accounting software, you can find company names to identify companies similar to your best clients. You can use email addresses to create lookalike audiences and conduct targeted email campaigns. (Hopefully you already have a segmented email database of customers and prospects.) The key is leveraging these internal resources to effectively reach and engage those target groups.

The importance of internal data lies in its ability to provide clarity and direction. It helps initiate activities like email marketing and social media campaigns more quickly and efficiently. It also enables you to utilize advanced tools such as AI and machine learning, which generate additional lists based on inputted data.

Internal Data's Role in Managing Leads

The lead data you collect and what you do with it are essential to the success of your marketing strategy and campaigns.

For B2B companies, it is vital to have a well-defined process in place to handle the numerous leads generated through the various marketing tactics we discussed previously in the book. This involves determining where you route leads, identifying the responsible parties, and storing the lead data effectively. Implementing a customer relationship management (CRM) system like Salesforce or HubSpot can streamline lead management and ensure data capture for future use.

For B2C companies that use e-commerce for online purchases, receiving leads involves integrating your online store with accounting and point-of-sale software, such as QuickBooks or SAP. This automation ensures that orders are processed seamlessly, inventory is updated, and the customer's journey is efficient. Depending on the complexity of your operations, you may require more sophisticated e-commerce platforms, such as Shopify or WooCommerce, to handle the entire order fulfillment process.

Benefits of Understanding Your Internal Data and Customer Insights

Based on the evaluation of your internal data and customer insights, you derive the following benefits to optimize your digital marketing efforts:

Data-driven decision making. The objective data you receive helps inform your marketing strategies and campaigns. Using internal data and customer insights ensures you make informed decisions instead of relying on guesswork.

Continuous improvement. Regularly assess your marketing initiatives and identify areas for improvement to refine your strategies and achieve better results.

Personalization and targeting. Leverage customer insights to create personalized and targeted marketing messages to increase relevance, engagement, and conversions.

Integration and automation. Integrating your marketing tools and systems to streamline processes ensures data consistency. Automation can help you efficiently manage leads, campaigns, and customer interactions.

Performance monitoring and analytics. Continuously monitoring and analyzing the performance of your marketing efforts will help you gain valuable insights into your campaign's effectiveness.

Conclusion

Understanding your internal data and customer insights is vital in optimizing digital marketing efforts. By understanding your inner resources, leveraging big data, and effectively managing leads, you can make data-driven decisions, enhance personalization, and improve overall performance.

Chapter 12
Assemble the Right Team

To successfully run your campaigns, you must assemble the right marketing team. This chapter describes how chief marketing officers and marketing directors can build the team to conduct successful digital marketing campaigns.

Assembling the right team starts with understanding who you currently have on staff, what they're best at, and what weaknesses exist that could create gaps you need to fill. That's easy for a small company. They have a marketing director. She is good at *X*, *Y*, and *Z* but doesn't know how to do web development, videography, graphic design, or whatever the need is now. In that case, it's obvious which gaps need to be filled. However, it's much less evident for a large company with marketing departments spanning many enterprise divisions.

Reviewing your workload and common requests (near term and short term) will help you identify your team's gaps

FTE vs. Freelance vs. Agency

The next step in assembling the team is deciding whether to fill the gap(s) with full-time employees (FTE), free-lancers, or agencies. Three factors come into play when choosing among these options:

Bandwidth Requirements

Bandwidth requirements relate to how much work needs to be filled by each specialty to execute your marketing strategy and campaign. How many hours per month by discipline do you have? Are they required for short-term projects, or do you need their support all year?

Budgets

Once you identify needed specialties, the budget becomes a consideration. Freelancers should cover short-term projects, while it may be more economical for FTEs or an agency to fill full-year support requirements.

For instance, a freelance videographer is much less expensive to hire once a month for three days than a full-time employee. However, if you need that freelancer a dozen times a month, hiring an FTE is less expensive because the freelancer's rates are typically higher.

Management Capabilities

Management capabilities comprise another area to consider. Do you have a marketing director or other in-house staff to supervise FTEs or freelancers? If not, then an agency might be your best choice.

What to Look for When Choosing an Agency

All agencies aren't created equal, so there are certain qualities to look for when hiring one:

- **Communication.** Ensure communication styles align.

- **Marketing practices.** Would you hire a marketing agency with a website that looks like it was built in 1995, doesn't have an active social media presence, or has never run a paid advertising campaign? The likelihood is that you would not. Instead, opt for an agency that practices what it preaches.

- **Process.** You want an agency that has established business and marketing processes. Some are highly creative, but everything is like spaghetti. They throw it on the wall to see if it sticks.

- **Portfolio.** Lastly, look for an agency with a strong portfolio (preferably in your industry) and solid case studies to back it up.

Support to Reach Your Marketing Goals

Knowing that your input, approvals, and direction will influence the campaign's success is essential whether you manage full-time employees, freelancers, or an agency. That is why we do not advise company CEOs or owners to manage marketing themselves. Typically, they lack the necessary expertise and time to ensure success. This tale of two CEOs illustrates our point.

Business Owner with Final Approval Standing in the Way

A family-owned business hired us to develop a new website for their construction company. They wanted to improve the visual appearance of the large-scale projects they were working on. Their entire digital presence, including their website, had not changed in about a decade, which made the company look old and out of business. In his early sixties, the company owner was disappointed that people didn't understand what they were working on. Nor did he comprehend how important the website was to the company's perception in the marketplace.

Your website is like the cover of a book—and people judge the book by its cover. So, with that frustration, we decided to help this client create a new digital presence, starting with their website and expanding into the other digital marketing areas we talk about in this book.

The owner had enough confidence in hiring our firm to put down a sizeable deposit and sign up for a monthly retainer. He also had a son who would presumably take over the business in the next several years to run the project.

Due to his young age, the owner's son had an excellent grasp of digital marketing, but he also had about ten years of business experience. He was smart and decisive, so right away we started working on updated brand and website concepts with custom imagery and messaging that would revolutionize how people perceived the company. He gave us some changes but approved the branding and website launch in a fashion that we're used to. We developed the website quickly, which was vital because we had a digital marketing and advertising strategy starting to roll out concurrently with the website update.

The father wanted to see the site before it went live. He stepped in at the last second and said, "This isn't going live because it doesn't look how I want it to." As a result the project stalled for over a year. (That is a prevalent problem because business owners get involved but don't have the capacity to stay involved.)

We talk about perfection getting in the way of progress all the time. The owner lacked the understanding that a website is never finished but an ongoing product that can be updated routinely. By not taking the site live, he also didn't realize that the company was losing an opportunity for leads, thus inhibiting growth. The existing digital campaigns had no site to tie back to. By not seeing the big picture, not understanding the process, and not being a marketing person, the owner was holding back the entire business from achieving success.

A Dedicated Point of Contact

The owner of a similar company contracted us to create a marketing campaign. This client had built and sold a construction company and had a successful exit, which he credited to digital marketing. When his noncompete was up, he started another company and called on our agency to build his digital presence.

Unlike his counterpart, the owner understood that he lacked the bandwidth to lead the project and hired a marketing director to oversee the company's marketing efforts. He recognized that the new hire was the best person to understand his brand and manage the company's growth goals.

For that reason we could move things along quicker and more efficiently, and they could give guidance regularly because they had the bandwidth to do so. The marketing director grasped the company's vision and goals and had the time to fine-tune our work to align with them, ensuring a greater chance for success. Although she had enough budget to hire a small internal team, she needed a nimble and highly qualified agency like ours to take the ball and run with it—and that's precisely what we did.

The key to their digital marketing success lay in the fact that the owner understood its importance and was willing to trust someone else to manage the process, and that person was smart enough to hire an agency to get everything up and running quickly. The company grew as a result and is still our client to this day. In fact, the CEO takes me around the country to speak at conventions and trade shows about our work for him.

Team Options

Now that you understand the importance of assembling the right team, how do you go about it? Whether you choose full-time employees or outsource to freelancers or an agency depends on the demand and frequency of work. But the positions you hire for typically fall into three tiers:

Tier 1—Minimal partial marketing role or full-time marketing manager/director

What we find best with a tier-one marketing department is a full-time marketing manager or director. If your budget does not allow for that, then it could be someone who has marketing experience and serves in a partial capacity, supported by freelancers or an agency to fill the gaps.

Typical tier 1 company profiles

- $3–$20 million in revenue
- 1–50 employees
- Moderate growth goals
- Little to no cyclical innovation in products or services

Tier 2—Marketing manager/director plus designer, copywriter, or coordinator

A tier-two would be the more mid-level support, involving a marketing manager or director plus a designer, copywriter, and/or a marketing coordinator in-house, supported by freelancers or an agency. Choosing between a designer, copywriter, or an additional coordinator depends on the need, goals, and gaps.

Typical tier 2 company profiles

- $12–$100 million in revenue
- 50+ employees
- Moderate to aggressive growth goals
- Little to no cyclical innovation in products or services

Tier 3—Enterprise—marketing department with several employees

Enterprise organizations will have a marketing department consisting of several full-time employees—30, 40, 50, or more—accompanied by various specialized agencies depending on need. (Enterprises seldom use freelancers.)

Typical tier 3 company profiles

- $100 million plus in revenue
- 200+ employees
- Moderate growth goals

Types of Positions

Here are positions you could consider based on the needs highlighted above:

Marketing Manager

Marketing managers are responsible for developing, implementing, and executing strategic marketing plans to attract and retain customers. They also manage marketing teams, plan strategies and budgets, liaise with clients, and track results.

Senior Web Developer

Senior web developers are skilled computer coding professionals responsible for designing, developing, and debugging the backend of software. They may also lead a team of junior web developers, manage complex projects, and work with UX to determine frontend user experience and website layout.

Junior Web Developer

Junior web developers are computer coding professionals responsible for small- to medium-sized programming tasks. They typically perform various tasks, including creating and maintaining websites, building landing pages, designing HTML emails and banner ads, and developing wireframes.

Creative Director

Creative directors are the creative leads in an organization. They determine the creative vision of a project, oversee the creative process (including strategy and campaign execution), and guide the creative department.

Art Director

Art directors use visuals to convey a company's desired image to consumers. They also manage graphic designers and artists, review work created by their team, develop concepts, and present designs for approval.

Graphic Designer

Graphic designers create visual concepts to communicate a company's desired image to consumers. They develop the overall layout of art and copy regarding arrangement, size, and other aesthetic concerns.

Junior Graphic Designer

Junior graphic designers perform visual design tasks. They may lay out website pages, create logos, rework text, and perform color corrections to enhance their skill set.

Videographer

Videographers shoot, develop, and edit videos. Their primary focus is to capture and record important moments as they happen.

Photographer

Photographers capture images of people, places, products, and events. They also edit photos to fit a company's desired vision and branding.

Photo/Video Post-Production

Post-production covers all stages of production occurring after a photo or video shoot. This may include editing, visual effects, feedback, music scoring, post-production sound, color correction, mastering, and more.

Digital Strategist or Coordinator

Digital strategists or coordinators are responsible for implementing various strategic marketing tactics (such as SEO, SEM, email marketing, etc.) to meet brand objectives based on consumer insights and data.

Social Media Strategist

Social media strategists develop social media campaigns, both organic and paid, based on a brand's goals and target audience. This includes deciding which platforms are best, how often a company posts, the type of content, and more.

Paid Media Strategist

Paid media strategists execute campaigns across various paid media platforms, including social media, CTV/OTT, and search engines. They are responsible for creating and launching ads that reach a company's target audience to increase brand awareness, website traffic, qualified leads, and more.

Senior Copywriter

Senior copywriters lead creative marketing content efforts. They are responsible for conceptualizing and developing a client's verbal or textual content and may oversee a copywriting team. They are focused on creatively conveying a client's message to generate sales.

Copywriter

Copywriters are also responsible for creating a client's verbal or textual content. They are focused on creatively conveying a client's message to generate sales and have a hand in many different mediums (social media, website, email, press releases, etc.)

Conclusion

Assembling the right marketing team begins by evaluating workload, capabilities gaps, and budget constraints. The best configuration depends on the complexity and consistency of requirements, leading to decisions about whether to hire full-time employees, contract freelancers, or outsource to an agency. Regardless of the configuration, qualified, well-aligned teams transform goals into reality by anticipating challenges and capitalizing on opportunities.

13

Chapter 13
Utilize the Power of AI

This chapter focuses on the integration of AI in today's digital marketing landscape. We review how AI can benefit your efforts, making *The Sharkbite Method*™ an even deadlier tactic for your business.

When I first contemplated the idea of integrating Artificial Intelligence (AI) into *The Sharkbite Method*™, a flurry of concerns clouded my judgment. As a staunch advocate for preserving the human touch in our campaigns, there was certainly a fear that AI would eliminate jobs and suppress the raw, intuitive creativity that our team was known for.

Just the thought of these soulless algorithms overshadowing human intellect initially deterred me from even considering AI as a valuable tool. However, as I delved deeper, my perspective began to shift. I discovered that AI wasn't the job-stealing, creativity-stifling monster I had imagined. On the contrary, it turned out to be an incredible asset.

It was already integrated into much of the software we utilize regularly, and by handling repetitive tasks and streamlining processes, it granted my team the luxury of time that they could now spend brainstorming, innovating, and pushing the boundaries of their creativity. What's more, I was pleasantly surprised by the "creative" solutions AI came up with based on data patterns and historical trends, allowing us to craft more resonant and impactful campaigns.

The integration of AI in the digital marketing landscape offers vast opportunities for optimization, personalization, and enhanced engagement. Harnessing its capabilities can provide a competitive edge and significantly augment marketing efforts. With that newfound knowledge, let's explore how AI can revolutionize various facets of digital marketing based on foundations and tactics from *The Sharkbite Method*™.

1. Creative Brief Development

Crafting a compelling creative brief is foundational. It's the blueprint that houses your brand's objectives, along with target audience insights and key messaging. A perfect brief sets the trajectory for a successful campaign.

AI applications:

- **Audience insights:** Tools like IBM Watson are revolutionary. They don't just provide surface-level demographics. By dissecting enormous volumes of consumer data, they unearth deep-seated behaviors, preferences, and tendencies, enabling marketers to tailor their campaigns with precision.

- **Messaging:** Every audience segment resonates differently with varying messages. AI streamlines this process, running rapid A/B tests on a plethora of messages to pinpoint what evokes the most potent response, ensuring higher engagement and conversion rates.

- **Visual preferences:** Platforms can transcend traditional analytics. By predicting creative performance, they allow marketers to select visual assets most likely to captivate their target demographic, enhancing overall campaign effectiveness.

- **Trend forecasting:** AI can identify emerging trends in your industry by analyzing vast datasets, allowing marketers to stay ahead of the curve and integrate upcoming themes into their campaigns. This ensures relevance and contemporary appeal in all marketing endeavors.

175

2. Content Calendar Creation

A strategic content calendar is like a compass in the vast ocean of digital media. It ensures direction, consistency, and timely engagement, acting as the backbone of an effective digital strategy.

AI applications:

- **Content suggestions:** With the internet overflowing with content, staying relevant is challenging. AI tools constantly monitor the digital pulse, identifying trending topics and keywords, ensuring your content is always in sync with what users are searching for.

- **Optimal posting time:** Beyond crafting perfect content, knowing when to release it is crucial. Using machine learning algorithms, AI tools analyze audience activity patterns, suggesting optimal times for posting and ensuring maximum visibility and engagement.

- **Performance predictors:** The future isn't entirely unpredictable. By analyzing historical data and juxtaposing it with current market trends, AI can fairly accurately predict how a piece of content might perform, guiding strategic adjustments.

- **Content curation:** Advanced AI tools, when combined with deep learning, can curate high-quality content suggestions based on the target audience's consumption patterns, making it easier for marketers to maintain a steady stream of relevant content.

3. Website Optimization

Your website is your digital storefront, a nexus between your brand and potential customers. In today's era, where first impressions often make or break deals, ensuring your website is optimized is nonnegotiable.

AI applications:

- **User experience (UX):** By meticulously analyzing user behavior, AI tools can highlight potential pain points in navigation or design, allowing businesses to enhance the overall user experience.

- **Chatbots:** More than just digital assistants, chatbots powered by natural language processing offer personalized user guidance, instant query resolution, and efficient lead generation around the clock. This not only enhances user experience but also boosts conversions.

- **Personalization:** Today's consumers expect tailor-made experiences. AI algorithms dynamically adjust website content, aligning with individual user behaviors and preferences, ensuring each visitor feels uniquely catered to.

- **Predictive analytics:** AI can anticipate user behavior based on past actions, allowing for predictive modifications. For instance, if a user often abandons an e-commerce shopping cart, AI might offer them a special discount or a reminder, increasing the chances of conversion.

4. Search Engine Marketing (SEM)

In the bustling digital marketplace, standing out is paramount. SEM offers that spotlight. Leveraging AI in SEM can ensure that this spotlight shines brighter and focuses more accurately on your target audience.

AI applications:

- **Keyword analysis:** Tools for keyword analysis are indispensable. By harnessing AI, they continually analyze search behaviors, suggesting high-performing keywords that can drive traffic and conversions.

- **Bid management:** The world of online ads is fast paced. Platforms use AI for real-time bid management, dynamically adjusting bids to ensure the best ROI on every penny spent.

- **Ad performance optimization:** AI tools analyze real-time engagement metrics, suggesting tweaks in ad creatives and copy to maximize effectiveness and engagement.

- **Ad copy optimization:** AI tools can analyze which ad copies or calls to action resonate best with the target audience and suggest modifications, thereby ensuring that ads not only reach the audience but also engage them effectively.

5. Social Media Marketing

The dynamism of social media platforms presents both opportunities and challenges. With the potential to reach billions, crafting an effective strategy rooted in insights and timely execution is vital.

AI applications:

- **Audience analysis:** AI tools offer a granular breakdown of audience segments, providing insights into which segments are most active, receptive, and engaging. This fine-tunes content strategy and ad targeting.

- **Content recommendations:** AI-powered tools can suggest content formats, optimal posting times, and even aesthetic elements like colors that resonate most with the audience.

- **Ad targeting:** AI's strength lies in real-time adaptability. By continually analyzing engagement data, AI tools can dynamically tweak ad targeting parameters to ensure the highest engagement and conversion rates.

- **Sentiment analysis:** AI algorithms can comb through social media platforms to gauge the sentiment around a brand or product. By understanding positive, negative, or neutral sentiments, brands can adjust their strategies to either capitalize on positivity or address concerns.

6. Email Marketing

The age-old tool of email marketing still holds significant sway in the digital realm. The key to success lies in personalization, timing, and resonance.

AI applications:

- **Personalization:** AI platforms can redefine email campaigns. By analyzing user behaviors, they allow for the crafting of personalized email content, dramatically boosting open and engagement rates.

- **Optimal send times:** It's not just about crafting the perfect email but sending it when it's most likely to be seen. AI tools analyze recipient behavior patterns to suggest optimal send times, maximizing the chances of engagement.

- **Subject line testing:** The first impression matters. AI tools can run multivariate tests on subject lines, gauging which ones are most likely to pique interest, leading to higher open rates.

- **Behavior-triggered emails:** Using AI, automated email campaigns can be initiated based on user behaviors. For instance, if a user reads an article about a particular product, an AI can trigger a follow-up email with a relevant offer or more information about that product.

7. CTV/OTT Media Buying

As the world gravitates toward CTV and OTT services, marketers are presented with uncharted territories that hold lots of potential. Navigating this space requires insights, precision, and timely adaptability.

AI applications:

- **Audience segmentation:** AI tools dive deep, identifying which shows, genres, or viewing patterns your target audience prefers, allowing for hyper-targeted ad placements.

- **Ad placement:** It's not just about reaching your audience but also reaching them at the right moment. AI can analyze viewing patterns, suggesting optimal ad lengths and precise placement within content streams to maximize viewer engagement and ad effectiveness.

- **Performance analysis:** Feedback loops are essential. AI offers real-time feedback on ad performance, allowing marketers to tweak strategies on the go, ensuring optimal returns on investment.

8. Measurement and Reporting

Navigating actionable insights among all your marketing data is crucial. AI acts as the compass, guiding marketers toward data-driven decisions that can shape future strategies.

AI applications:

- **Automated dashboards:** Dashboard reporting has been redefined. By pulling in real-time data, they present visual insights, enabling quick decisions and strategic moves.

- **Predictive reporting:** Beyond just reporting on past and current metrics, AI can be employed to predict future trends based on historical data. This forward-looking perspective can be invaluable for strategizing upcoming campaigns and making informed budgeting decisions.

Conclusion

AI and digital marketing go hand in hand. As we've already explored, integrating AI across *The Sharkbite Method*™ can help to improve strategy, execution, and results. In a dynamic digital landscape, embracing AI ensures that marketers remain agile, insightful, and ahead of the curve.

Conclusion

"The best time to plant a tree was twenty years ago. The second-best time is now."—Anonymous

My hope is that *The Sharkbite Method*™ we discussed in this book will be implemented and *Make a Brand Impact*™!

I would like you to consider this: What would your business look like today had you applied *The Sharkbite Method*™ one year ago? Or even five years ago?

- Would more of your target audience know your brand?

- Would that brand awareness turn into top-line revenue?

- Would your growth goals, client retention rate, and company culture all be In a better spot?

Now imagine your business's potential if you began implementing the insights from this book today. If you started assembling the right team to build awareness and generate leads, had a creative brief that positioned your company properly, and had a strategic plan that you executed daily, weekly, and monthly. In this vision, how many more people would know about your brand, and where would it be in one year from now? Where would your company be in five years from now if you started today?

If you dived deep into your customer insights and managed your internal data meticulously, ensuring it's both segmented and detailed, and if you've consistently monitored your employees to guarantee data entry, how much data would you currently have? And how much of that data could you leverage to foster and expand your business?

It's never too late to start. Time flies and the digital marketing clock keeps ticking.

Start today if you aren't already working on your marketing strategy and plans while reading this book. Make the time. Put it in your schedule. It will redefine your business, its culture, and how people think about your brand. It could also have a profound effect on your personal life trajectory.

I am thrilled to have shared this comprehensive methodology with you. Over the years, I have witnessed many marketing challenges and frustrations. Yet, its solution is simple: Understand who you are and then let everyone else know. *The Sharkbite Method*™ is your playbook to do just that.

Harness the power of digital marketing and let your brand's voice resonate in your customers' and prospects' hearts and minds. The future is bright. It's time to take your bite!

Interested in applying *The Sharkbite Method*™ to your business? Get started here.

About the Author

Nick Kraus is an accomplished entrepreneur and business leader, serving as the Founder and CEO of Kraus Marketing, an award-winning agency known for its exceptional marketing strategy and creative. He started this company with a passion for marketing, business success, and to create a work culture focused around people who love what they do. Under Nick's strategic guidance, Kraus Marketing has achieved remarkable success, earning a place on the esteemed Inc 5000 list multiple times.

In addition to his role at Kraus Marketing, Nick is a recognized thought leader in the marketing and business community, providing valuable guidance to professionals seeking to stay ahead in the ever-evolving business landscape. His ability to articulate complex ideas and provide practical advice inspires and empowers businesses to achieve their goals through strategic marketing initiatives.

About the Company

Founded in 2004, Kraus Marketing is your all-in-one full-service digital marketing agency with offices in Morristown, NJ, Manhattan, NY, and Tampa, FL. Kraus Marketing specializes in branding, videography, web design and development, and an array of strategic digital marketing services. With a talented in-house team, Kraus Marketing quickly became the agency of choice for small to midsize businesses in need of innovative marketing solutions, but over the years, it has expanded to include enterprise-level companies.

Kraus Marketing strives to continually deliver exceptional work to each client, which requires staying on top of industry advancements. Learning is encouraged both inside and outside the office so that employees can participate in relevant coursework, obtaining proper certifications and pertinent skills. The result yields high-end marketing that produces the best ROI for your business.

Kraus Marketing is an award-winning agency that has received acknowledgments from Inc. 5000, NJBIZ Best Places to Work, American Inhouse Design, GDUSA, and more.

Notes

Notes

Interested in applying *The Sharkbite Method*™
to your business? Get started here.

Made in the USA
Las Vegas, NV
21 September 2024